Jam

6 9

Boston, Mass

BEACON HILL

Its Ancient Pastures and Early Mansions

DAVID SEARS MANSION AS ORIGINALLY BUILT ON THE SITE OF COPLEY'S RESIDENCE

41 AND 42 BEACON STREET

Portion of H. G. Otis house at left

BEACON HILL

Its Ancient Pastures and Early Mansions

BY

ALLEN CHAMBERLAIN

With Illustrations

BOSTON AND NEW YORK

HOUGHTON MIFFLIN COMPANY

The Riverside Press Cambridge

1925

The Riverside Press
CAMBRIDGE · MASSACHUSETTS
PRINTED IN THE U.S.A.

ACKNOWLEDGMENT

THESE studies of the older real estate ownerships of Beacon Hill were originally made for the 'Boston Evening Transcript,' and were published by that paper in 1923, 1924 and 1925 as a series of sixteen illustrated articles. In spite of due diligence in the collection of the facts, and notwithstanding painstaking efforts to avoid typographical errors, some inaccuracies of statement were inadvertently included in the original papers. Those papers are here reproduced only after careful revision, partially in the light of subsequent information, several of the chapters having been rewritten or expanded.

Without the inspiring and whole-hearted assistance given the writer by many recognized authorities on various aspects of the problems involved in these researches, the result would have been far less satisfactory. Most appreciative acknowledgment of their aid is therefore made to Julius H. Tuttle, Librarian, and to Worthington C. Ford, Editor, of the Massachusetts Historical Society; to Samuel Eliot Morison, historian, biographer of Harrison Gray Otis; to Walter K. Watkins, high authority on Boston antiquarian lore; to William Sumner Appleton, Corresponding Secretary of the Society

ACKNOWLEDGMENT

for the Preservation of New England Antiquities; to the late Irwin C. Cromack, long in the engineering service of the city of Boston; to John H. Edmonds, Curator of the State Archives; to Edward H. McGlenen, City Registrar; to the Reverend Charles A. Place, authority on the work of Charles Bulfinch; to Ellen Mudge Burrill, compiler of the Historical Notes on the State House; to the officers of the Bostonian Society, of the City Assessing Department, of the Boston Public Library, of the Boston Athenæum; to many representatives of those families early associated with the development of the west slope pastures; and to George S. Mandell, Managing Editor of the 'Boston Transcript,' for his encouragement of the undertaking.

The sources of information from which the facts here presented were drawn were the Suffolk Registry of Deeds, the files of the Suffolk Probate Office, the original assessment books of the Boston Assessors, the plan files of the Street Department of Boston, the private letter and document files of H. G. Otis, through the courtesy of their owner, the manuscript abstracts of title prepared by Nathaniel Ingersoll Bowditch during his long practice as a conveyancer (now in the library of the Massachusetts Historical Society), the 'Gleaner' papers by Bowditch in the Fifth Report of the Boston Record Commissioners, the original assess-

ACKNOWLEDGMENT

ment rolls relating to the United States tax on dwelling houses in 1798 (now in the library of the New England Historic-Genealogical Society), the Boston Directory (a full set in the library of the Bostonian Society), and certain private diaries and letter-books of the early nineteenth century to which access was generously given by the present owners.

CONTENTS

ILLUSTRATIONS

ILLUSTRATIONS

ILLUSTRATIONS

ILLUSTRATIONS

BEACON HILL

Its Ancient Pastures and Early Mansions

BEACON HILL

I

FENCE–VIEWING IN THE ANCIENT PASTURES

DURING the summer and autumn of 1855 the 'Boston Evening Transcript' published a series of articles dealing with the history of real estate titles in Boston, and chiefly concerning those on and around Beacon Hill. The author, who signed himself 'Gleaner,' was Nathaniel Ingersoll Bowditch, a son of the distinguished mathematician, Dr. Nathaniel Bowditch, and himself the best-informed and leading conveyancing lawyer of the city in his day. Those papers are classic and are recognized by all antiquaries as furnishing the most complete and dependable information as to the ancient ownerships, and as to the development of the Hill, anywhere to be found. Happily they have been preserved in convenient form through their republication by the Boston Record Commissioners in 1880 as a city document.

In those chapters, which were written in a familiar epistolary vein, Mr. Bowditch went into considerable detail as to owners, past and present, with side-lights upon their family connections and standing in the community. He also gave liberal citations to such public records as Suffolk Deeds and the Probate files, and in his descriptions of the old land boundaries he most illuminatingly tied them in with references to the existing landmarks of his day, such as street lines and the residences of persons at that time well known in the city. The present-day reader of those pages will be frequently confused, however, by many unfamiliar street names — for there have been changes in the nomenclature of the Hill since 1855 — unless he makes reference to that other valuable public document, the work of Irwin C. Cromack and William H. Macmann, of the city engineering service, and published by the Street Commissioners in 1910 as 'A Record of the Streets, Alleys, Places, etc., in the City of Boston.' And unless the reader is a Hillite of long standing, or one familiar with the history of its old families, no reference to a modern real estate atlas will enable him to locate the properties alluded to by Mr. Bowditch by the names of the owners in his day.

The accompanying map, covering the old Trimountain with its three summits, shows the present-day streets and alleys from Cambridge Street on the north to the Common on the south, and from Scollay Square on the east to Charles Street on the west. Upon this there have been plotted in heavily accented lines the boundaries of

THE ANCIENT PASTURE FENCE LINES AS THEY WOULD APPEAR IF REBUILT THROUGH THE STREETS
AND HOUSES OF 1925

Heavy lines represent old property boundaries. Original three summits indicated by hachure, with old Town Plot on Beacon Hill

the old properties as they existed prior to the Revolutionary War, or as nearly as the writer has been able to interpret the Bowditch descriptions of those properties. Minutely detailed as were the delineations of the several parcels in the Bowditch text, with measurements often down to inches, his compass courses were only generalized, and there are apparently discrepancies in some of the distances given, due in some instances, perhaps, to typographical errors. In many cases the measurements are only given for one or two sides of a property, the remaining boundaries being described in more or less graphic general terms. An effort has been made to check up on some of the ambiguous features by reference to the file of ancient plans in the Street Laying-Out Department of the city, to recorded plans in the Registry of Deeds, and to Bowditch's original title abstracts in fifty-five ledger volumes. In this way more than one bafflingly indefinite fence line has been located within an acceptable degree of precision. The map makes no pretension to being an accurate plan of the ancient holdings on the Hill, but is merely an attempt to interpret 'Gleaner's' descriptions of the properties with as great a degree of faithfulness as the material at hand would permit.

Other attempts have been made in the past to map the real estate subdivisions of the old town. The late George Lamb, of Cambridge, a retired sea

3

captain with antiquarian tastes, and the late
Uriel H. Crocker, of Boston, a prominent conveyancer, both undertook the task, and the Lamb map
was purchased by the city in 1879 and is now in
the custody of the Public Library. But whereas
the Bowditch descriptions are confined in the main
to Beacon Hill, and deal with ownerships for the
most part of the eighteenth century, the other
gentlemen covered the entire town as it was in its
earliest days, drawing their data from the Book of
Possessions, wherein the forefathers recorded their
land conveyances. In a number of instances the
ownerships described by Bowditch follow the lines
of the original town grants, but in other cases his
boundaries represent subsequent consolidations of
several smaller pieces, for land speculation seems
to have been more or less rampant even among the
clergy of those 'good old days.'

What was known as Beacon Hill in the olden
times was a definitely limited area covering the
main summit of Trimountain, now for the most
part included within the State House grounds.
During the past hundred years or more the name
has come to embrace not only the decapitated
summit, but its slopes as well, or that part, at least,
bounded by Somerset Street on the east, by Charles
River Basin on the west, and from Cambridge
Street to the Common. Where once were sunny
pastures, bits of tillage and orchards, there is now

4

a dense population with business in possession of much of the eastern slope with occasional encroachments elsewhere, the remainder being in dwellings old and new, fashionable and otherwise. It is a little town in itself, presenting a social cross-section of the city as a whole. Although scarce a trace remains of its provincial landmarks — only an ancient fence line here and there being still preserved in part by présent-day party boundaries — many of the houses contemporaneous with the State House yet remain, and not a few of the descendants of the families who developed the Hill nearly a century and a quarter ago continue to live there. From the settlement in 1630 until after the Revolution, the Hill suffered little physical change. Along the eastern and northeastern fronts, on Tremont Street and Tremont Row, and on Court Street, houses were early built. On the Beacon Street front, opposite the Common, there were three or four country seats, such as the Copley and Hancock places. There were also some attempts at house-lot development on the northerly and northwest sides before the middle of the eighteenth century, but without much success. The rest was mainly pasture ground where cattle and horses grazed among the blueberry and barberry bushes, or lolled in the hot days under the shade of the elms and cedars. The era of marked transformation opened with the building of the State House in

1795, and continued through the next fifty years, during which period the Hill was shorn of its characteristic summits, one by one, and close-packed streets overran the pastures.

About the earliest published description of Boston is found in William Wood's 'New England Prospects,' printed in London in 1634. In the course of his narrative he speaks of the hills as follows: 'At one corner, a great broad hill whereon is planted a Fort, which can command any ship as she sayles into any Harbour within the still Bay. On the North-side is another Hill equal in bignesse, whereon stands a Winde-mill. To the North-west is a high Mountaine with three little rising Hills on the top of it, wherefore it is called the "Tramount."' Obviously these are Fort, Copp's, and Beacon Hills, and, in spite of the definiteness of Wood's statement, many Bostonians persist in believing that they gave rise to our word 'Tremont.' Old pictures of the town, as it was seen in early days from the Charlestown shore, show the three summits of Trimountain clearly. Sentry Hill, as it was first known, later Beacon, rose as a shapely central cone perhaps sixty feet higher than the base of the present monument. From this crest a ridge swung easterly, just back of Beacon Street, and terminated in another but slightly lower eminence, known as Cotton Hill on the Court-House site, at the foot of which dwelt the Reverend John Cotton.

From the western foot of the main summit cone another ridge stretched out toward the Charles, and this in turn rose to another summit at a point between Pinckney and Mount Vernon Streets, and just above Louisburg Square. At various times this latter knob bore a variety of names, but the name of Mount Vernon eventually became supreme.

Between 1801 and 1805, Mount Vernon was graded down for house lots, the gravel going into the river to make the land over which Charles Street was laid out. In 1811, the town sold its public plot of six rods square, that was originally set aside as a beacon site by act of the General Court in 1634-35, and on which a monument, of which the present one is a reproduction, was erected in 1790. The purchasers at once set about reducing the hill to the general level of the State House, and eventually Temple Street was extended across the site as far as Mount Vernon Street, and more or less as the footway now runs along the easterly side of the State House extension. That left the ridge on the east and Cotton Hill as the only remnants of the old Trimountain. In 1835, the Pemberton Square real estate development was begun by a syndicate, and so Cotton Hill was dug down and carted away. Asa G. Sheldon, who was the contractor on this work, has left an interesting account of the undertaking in his autobiography. He stated that the elevation of the hill was reduced by sixty-

7

five feet. From that it is assumed that Cotton Hill was about twenty feet lower than Beacon Hill. After another ten years the ridge that connected the two summits was itself smoothed away, thus completing the topographical remodeling of Trimountain.

In his descriptions of the ancient pasture ownerships of the hill Mr. Bowditch began at the foot of the northwest slope, near the junction of Cambridge and Charles Streets, and worked easterly along the north slope to Cotton Hill, thence swinging around and down the southerly side to the river again. Reference to the map will show that the original beach line along the river front was wholly east of Charles Street, and that from near what is now the easterly approach to the West Boston Bridge a deep cove made up into the land to a little east of Anderson Street. At the mouth of this cove begins a pasture which, in 1658, was bought by Zacariah Phillips, butcher. It extended southerly along the bluff above the beach to an undetermined point somewhere between Pinckney and Mount Vernon Streets, where it came in contact with William Blaxton's six-acre piece. The easterly boundary of this lot, and the right-angle jog near Louisburg Square, were described by Bowditch with great particularity, leaving as admittedly indeterminate the two hundred feet or so of south boundary which ran 'westerly to the sea.' In his private title abstracts, however, there is a plan upon which he essayed to lay down this doubtful boundary, but with a notation reading, 'Probable south boundary of Phillips.' The lines on the plan of the old pastures follow that interpretation of the title. This pasture was sold to Governor John Leverett in 1672, from whom it descended to his heirs, and by whom the northerly end was laid out into house lots in 1729 in conjunction with a similar development then being carried out by the Allen family on the adjoining pasture. These were the earliest attempts to promote a systematic dwelling scheme on the west side of the Hill, but it evidently succeeded poorly, and the neighborhood acquired anything but a savory reputation. The thick-walled structure shown on the plan by dotted lines as straddling Pinckney Street just above West Cedar was a public powder house built in 1770 with a capacity of a thousand barrels. Its location is shown on a plan of 1796 [1] at the Registry, and another small structure, shown a hundred feet or so east of it, is presumed to have been the watch house. In 1802, the Legislature ordered the demolition of this magazine, whereupon it was purchased by the Mount Vernon Proprietors, who tore it down prior to 1804 and used the materials in their grading operations. [2] The position of

[1] Suffolk Deeds, L. 192, f. 198. (Subsequent citations of this nature are from the same source unless otherwise stated.)
[2] H. G. Otis's 'Memorandum of Title.' Otis Papers.

the powder house assumed great importance in a suit brought, in 1836, against the purchasers of the Copley title by the Overseers of the Poor of Boston, claiming rights under the will of Benjamin Pemberton, of Roxbury, to portions of the Copley property. The Mount Vernon Proprietors asserted title to the southerly end of the old Phillips pasture, their claim being based upon the proved fact that the fence along the Copley north border had for many years been attached to the powder house and ran thence straight down to the water. Some one at some time, inadvertently it is to be hoped, had enclosed more than was lawfully his, and in the absence of protest by the other owner had acquired the semblance of a title through the lapse of years.

The next property on that side Bowditch called the James Allen pasture. The Reverend Mr. Allen evidently believed firmly in the future worth of West End real estate, and during the closing decade of the seventeenth century he began picking up parcels, both north and south of Cambridge Street, or of the lane to the pastures, as it was then known. Bit by bit he thus acquired twenty acres on the north side of Cambridge Street, and sixteen on the south. This latter extended from the Phillips land easterly to Irving Street and southerly into the middle of Mount Vernon Street. This pasture was supposed to contain in all sixteen and a half acres and was acquired in three purchases between 1696 and 1699. The first was the large area fronting on Cambridge Street, reaching to just south of Myrtle Street. South of that was an interior lot, originally a part of the Phillips pasture, but reserved by Samuel Cole when he sold the latter. This Allen added to the first. Another interior lot of two acres or more adjoining the Cole tract on the east, and lying between Mount Vernon Street and Myrtle, was also his. This last bit was originally a part of a larger pasture belonging first to Zaccheus Bosworth. Sometime subsequent to 1665 it was bought by Humphrey Davie, a lawyer, as a country place. Mr. Davie's town house was opposite King's Chapel Burying Ground, and was later known as the residence of the Faneuil family. Old maps indicate that he had a house close to Mount Vernon Street just below Joy, and that there was also an orchard on the lot that Mr. Bowditch was inclined to believe was the one planted by Blaxton prior to 1630. The plan of 1796 in the Registry, already alluded to, includes this lot and shows the lines of an old roadway leading from its southeast corner toward the State House. It is known that there was an ancient roadway called Davie's Lane running from opposite the head of Park Street athwart the slope of Beacon Hill to the ridge of Mount Vernon, and its approximate lines are shown on the accompanying plan. Deeds as far back as 1735 also refer to a highway here which had by that time come to be known as Olive Street.

Between Irving and Hancock Streets, and running back to the south side of Myrtle, was the Thomas Buttolph eight-and-a-half-acre pasture. It continued in the ownership of this family for many years until the grandchildren of Thomas, one of whom was Mrs. Joseph Belknap, Jr., laid out streets and began selling lots. Joy Street, from Cambridge to Myrtle, was cut through Mrs. Belknap's portion and was originally known as Belknap's Lane. A ropewalk across its Myrtle Street end effectually prevented its being extended over the hill to join the section running south from Mount Vernon into Beacon Street, and then known as George Street, until about 1800. Irving Street was known as Buttolph Street until 1855.

The next four-acre lot was perhaps an original grant to the Scottow family, for Thomas sold it to his brother Joshua in 1648. In 1691, it having passed into other hands, the pasture was divided into east and west halves and sold again, Stephen Minot buying the westerly two acres, and Isaiah Tay the easterly portion. According to Mr. Bowditch it extended from the west side of Hancock Street to the west side of the alley east of Temple Street, and ran back up the hill to what is now Derne Street at the foot of the Beacon Hill cone. Tay's heirs laid out Temple Street, and it bore his

name until 1769, when it was renamed for Sir John
Temple, son-in-law of James Bowdoin, who was
afterward Governor of the Commonwealth. Mr.
Minot sold a portion of his end that came into possession of Joseph Ridgway in 1768, and he laid out
the lane which has since borne his name.

From the Scottow east line on Cambridge Street
to the westerly side of the old Revere House lot in
Bowdoin Square, and extending southerly to the
foot of Beacon Hill, lay the four acres called by
Bowditch the Middlecott pasture. This Richard
Middlecott bought in 1677 and it remained in his
family until after his heirs cut it up in 1727, laying
out Middlecott Street, subsequently renamed for
Governor Bowdoin, who lived close to its junction
with Beacon Street. Some of this land, on the
Cambridge Street front, east of Bowdoin Street,
was bought in 1757 by Harrison Gray, the Treasurer of the Province, and grandfather of Harrison
Gray Otis, Sr. Joseph Coolidge also bought a large
section on the westerly corner of Bowdoin and
Cambridge Streets and built a mansion house surrounded with a handsome garden.

Next came a pasture lot of four acres that belonged to the grandfather of Charles Bulfinch, Dr.
Thomas Bulfinch, who lived just across the way on
the Court Street side of Bowdoin Square. He
bought it of Samuel Lynde, who had inherited it
from his grandfather, John Newgate, who was

probably the first possessor. At one time Lynde bought the lot adjoining this on the south, and running from Ashburton Place through to Beacon Street. Subsequently he sold the Beacon Street frontage, but retained a piece on the Ashburton Street end as an addition to the Cambridge Street pasture. And right here is to be found one of those old fence lines that remain visible on the face of the Hill to-day. Where the Bulfinch east line crossed what is now Ashburton Place, just east of the Boston University Law School, the pasture abutted upon the back land of the Reverend John Cotton, whose dwelling was between Tremont Row and Pemberton Square. Bulfinch wrote in this connection that 'The west line of Cotton's estate coincides with the east line of Bulfinch's pasture, i.e., of the Church estate in Ashburton Place.' The Law School building was formerly the Mount Vernon Church.

The next adjoining parcel contained two acres, but they were laid out in the form of an L. The land fronted on Court Street one hundred and seventy feet, ran south up what was known as Valley Acre, following more or less the east side of Somerset Street, but between Allston Street and Ashburton Place it turned sharply to the east, climbed over the top of Cotton Hill, and descended to Tremont Row, where it had a frontage of one hundred and three feet. According to the Book of

Possessions, Edward Bendall was the first owner, and he is credited with a house and two acres. In 1645, he sold to David Yeale. Few would suspect from the spelling of this name that David was the father of Elihu Yale, the benefactor of the University that bears his name. It is believed that Elihu was born in this Boston house in 1649. In 1653, Yeale sold to Captain John Wall, who, about 1655, rented some portion of it to Governor John Endicott as a habitation. Endicott lived on the Tremont Row slope of Cotton Hill. After Wall's death his heirs sold to Edward Shippen, and in 1702 the title to all except two small pieces on the north front came into the possession of Captain Cyprian Southack, a chart-maker, and Bowditch referred to the property as Southack's pasture. In 1720 he laid out Howard Street, calling it Southack Court.

The corner east and north of the Southack lot, and fronting on Court Street and Tremont Row, contained several small residence properties. Here dwelt Simon Lynde, once the owner of the Bulfinch pasture, his house being on the corner opposite the head of Sudbury Street. Lynde's daughter Elizabeth married George Pordage, whose only daughter, Hannah, married James Bowdoin and became mother of the Governor. Theodore Lyman the elder lived on a piece of this land south of Howard Street after 1785. Next south was the Tremont

15

Row end of the Southack lot where Governor Endicott lived, with Cotton Hill rising steeply behind.

Mr. John Cotton's 'one house and garden and about half an acre, with an acre adjoining,' as the Book of Possessions describes the property, fronted on what is now Scollay Square, and reached westerly up along the slope of Cotton Hill and on to the ridge connecting it with Beacon Hill, very irregular on its south line, and narrowing to one hundred and eighteen feet where it butted against the Bulfinch fence beside the Law School building on Ashburton Place. Here lived Mr. Cotton, and beside him, for a brief space, there dwelt the unfortunate Sir Harry Vane, the 'boy Governor.' About 1664, a portion of this land was sold to John Hull, the mint master, and this was inherited by his daughter, the wife of Judge Sewall, but the Sewall family did not live there. In 1758, it passed out of that family, and in 1803, it was bought by Gardiner Greene, son-in-law of John Singleton Copley, the painter, who developed it in connection with other lands there into a beautiful garden estate, the show place of the town. After his death, in 1832, it was bought by Patrick Jackson and others who cut down Cotton Hill and laid out Pemberton Square.

Adjoining the Cotton lot, at the corner of Pemberton Square and Tremont Street, there was the house of the Reverend Daniel Maud, then, 1635, a schoolmaster, but shortly thereafter pastor of the

16

church at Dover, New Hampshire. Next door, to the south, was a lot owned by Governor Bellingham. He sold a small piece next to Maud's to the Reverend John Davenport in 1670. The remaining portion, which ran back nearly to Somerset Street, Bellingham had already sold, in 1663, to Humphrey Davie, who built a stone house there which, in 1710, Davie's heirs sold to Andrew Faneuil, uncle of the famous Peter. Mr. Davie, it will be recalled, had also a retired suburban home on the ridge of Mount Vernon, not far from Joy Street. Just before the Revolution the property was acquired by John Vassal, a loyalist, and in 1783, the State confiscated it.

John Coggan, the first keeper of a shop in the town, was the earliest possessor of the adjoining little lot, and at his death it was described as his orchard. This, like its neighbors on either hand, is now engulfed in the Houghton & Dutton building. Later it was owned by the Reverend John Oxenbridge, pastor of the First Church. First and last this bit of Tremont Street was, therefore, the home of four clergymen. Then on the corner of Beacon Street — early known as the 'Lane to the Almshouse' — there was the home of James Penn, ruling elder of the church, and next above him on Beacon Street lived the Reverend James Allen, whose real estate investments on the north of the Hill have been referred to. He was related to the Penn family.

17

The property was held by the Allen family until 1810, when it came into the possession of David Hinckley who built a double stone house on the lot. This later became the first home of the Somerset Club, and subsequently, and for some years, the headquarters of the Congregational Society.

A pasture described by Mr. Bowditch as 'of a most peculiar triangular shape,' with a frontage of only thirteen feet six inches on Beacon Street, all but blocked the present entrance to Somerset Street. Its lines are readily traced in a plan made when Somerset Street was laid out, and now in the archives of the Street Laying-Out Department of the city.[1] It is also recognizable in a plan in the Bowditch abstracts.[2] This Bowditch called the James Davis or Major Thompson two-acre pasture. James Davis was the owner in 1659–60, but it fell into the hands of Major Robert Thompson, of London, soon after 1677, and it descended as an entailed estate for eighty years, when, the entail being barred, the property was sold, and at last came into possession of John Bowers, of Somerset, Massachusetts, who laid out Somerset Street.

Robert Turner was an early investor in Beacon Hill realty. In all he acquired about eight acres, most of which lay along the south slope of the ridge above Beacon Street as far west as the head of

[1] Boston Street Commissioner's ancient plans, vol. 1, p. 20.
[2] Bowditch Abstracts, vol. 6, p. 354.

Park Street. At that point his land bounded on a thirty-foot public way leading to the beacon, more or less on the lines of the present foot-passage to and through the East Wing of the State House, and substantially as shown on the map. The remainder of his holdings surrounded the summit of the Hill, abutting upon the Scottow pasture on the north, running west to within nineteen feet of Hancock Street, and following in a general way the line of Mount Vernon Street, where it passes under the State House archway, on the south. On the very top of the Hill an area six rods square had been reserved as a beacon site since 1634–35, and this Turner's land seems to have surrounded. Incidentally Turner was sergeant of the colonial militia, and because of this fact, and by reason of his near-by dwelling, it has been assumed by some that he may have been the first warden in charge of the beacon. His son-in-law, John Fairweather, eventually came to own much of this property. In 1742, David Sears, Sr., bought a house site nearest Somerset Street, and Edward Bromfield at the same time bought the lot next west. James Bowdoin took up the land west of that and along Bowdoin Street in 1756, and in 1760, William Molineaux bought where now the East Wing of the State House turns toward Beacon Street. The Bromfield house, that stood opposite the Athenæum, was taken down in 1845, when the ridge behind it was razed. The

Bowdoin house, on the site of the Bellevue and the Unitarian Association, was demolished two years earlier. Daniel Dennison Rogers bought the Molineaux property in 1782 and built a new house which remained until 1833. Mr. Molineaux, by the way, was a stanch patriot, but C. W. Apthorp, who inherited the house, was a loyalist, and the property was sold by the State to Mr. Rogers, who subsequently laid out the upper end of Bowdoin Street.

Next west of the old right of way to the beacon the boundary lines of the map show the extent of the Hancock property. Zaccheus Bosworth and Thomas Millard were original owners of the land between the street to the beacon and Joy Street, and thence northerly nearly to Mount Vernon Street. Any one who is interested in the intricacies of this title will be abundantly repaid by reading the six 'Gleaner' chapters dealing therewith. Most readers in this day and generation will be satisfied with the story as it applied to the Hancock family. Thomas Hancock, Governor John's wealthy uncle, made his first purchase on the Hill in 1735. This lot 'fronted on the Common' one hundred and thirty-five feet four inches. Here, where the bronze memorial plate is affixed to the State House fence, he built his stone house. For this land he paid one thousand pounds in provincial currency. In 1752, he added a pasture lot on the east and north

which carried his boundaries in the one direction as
far as the street to the beacon, and in the other
around on the westerly side of the town's six-rod
reservation almost to Derne Street, and to within
nineteen feet of Hancock Street on the west. This
latter portion will doubtless be recognized as a part
of the former holding of Robert Turner. His final
purchase was made in 1759, when he carried his
holdings westerly so as to bound on an ancient
lane, which now, in widened form, is known as Joy
Street. This piece, like his original house site, ran
north almost to Mount Vernon Street, or, in other
words, to a portion of Davie's Lane, the easterly
section of which once ran across his house site and
pasture to Park Street.

Before moving down Beacon Street further, it
will be necessary to stroll up that rustic lane along
the Hancock west fence as far as Mount Vernon
Street. There the cart-path emerged in a two-and-
a-half-acre pasture at a point seventy-seven feet
east of the Humphrey Davie orchard lot. In 1648
Zaccheus Bosworth owned both the Davie piece
and the one into which the lane led, and at one time
his land extended south to the Common, but in
1661, when that front land was parted with, the
family reserved a right of way ten feet wide from
Beacon Street to the remaining property on the
ridge. Richard Cooke bought the two and a half
acres in 1665, and his grandson, Elisha, who in-

herited the property, laid out Hancock Street across it, calling it after the former owner, Sergeant Turner, but this name was shortly changed to George and became Hancock in 1788. Cooke also carried Joy Street northerly toward Myrtle, about 1735, but, as has already been seen, the ropewalk across it at Myrtle made this piece a blind alley.

Westerly from Joy Street, Judge Samuel Sewall bought a pasture lot in 1692 comprising in all four and three-quarter acres. It extended westerly to the west entrance of the Somerset Club, 43 Beacon Street, and northerly into the middle of Mount Vernon Street, the northwest corner being directly in front of the Club of Odd Volumes, and was commonly known as Sewall's elm pasture. After his death his heirs thought that it might sell better if cut up into lots, and so proceeded to lay out three streets through it as shown by the dotted lines on the plan. Those streets probably never progressed beyond the staking-out stage. In 1770 and 1773, the westerly portion of this land was bought by Copley, the painter, as a part of the 'farm' that he was at that time acquiring, and it was on this portion of the property that his house stood. The easterly portion of the pasture was bought by Dr. John Joy in 1791, his boundaries being substantially Beacon, Joy, Mount Vernon, and Walnut Streets. Near his southeasterly corner he built his house, which remained until 1833.

Francis East appears to have been the original owner of the lot next west of Sewall's, the earliest evidence of his ownership being found in a deed of 1667 wherein he is named as an abutter. Eleven years later he petitioned the town authorities for a record title to his 'tract of land containing about 3 acres . . . which was formerly a towne grant . . . having been long in possession of said East.' And it was so entered upon the town records. On the Beacon Street front it reached, according to Bowditch, 'to just about the east line of Spruce Street,' and its westerly boundary ran back up the slope to old Mount Vernon almost to its crest, crossing Mount Vernon Street through the middle of the Theological School building, and extending north of that street about twenty-five or thirty feet. The northwest corner of the East lot was very close to the southeast corner of the house now numbered 87 Mount Vernon Street, at which point it made a junction with the Blaxton and Brattle (Allen) pastures. This pasture was sold to Thomas Bannister after East's death in 1694, at which time, according to the deed of conveyance, there was a house on it, and, in 1770, Copley added it to his farm.

Finally, at the foot of the hill, there was the homestead lot of the Reverend William Blaxton, the first settler of Boston. This spelling of his name is unfamiliar, but it was his own, as is witnessed by his signatures upon the records of Emmanuel College, at Cambridge, England, on the occasions when he received his degrees. Some three years after the coming of Winthrop and his company, at Mr. Blaxton's invitation, to live on this side the Charles, the colony took a formal title from Blaxton to the entire peninsula excepting fifty acres which he reserved for his own. Naturally these reserved lands were at the foot of Mount Vernon where he had his house. Then a year later he sold to the town all but six acres close to his house, by which act the people of Boston came into possession of the Common at a cost of thirty pounds.

No one knows where his house stood, but historical authorities seem to agree in the belief that it was somewhere on the slope back of Beacon Street and not far from Spruce Street. Nor is the location of his spring known to a certainty, but here again students of local history incline to the opinion that it may have been the one which was flowing copiously, even as lately as at the beginning of the last century, and the approximate position of which is indicated on the plan by a cross within the grassed enclosure of Louisburg Square. That particular spring, by the way, is said to have been highly prized by the colored washwomen of the Hill in former years as furnishing the best water in the region for their purposes. If Blaxton lived, as supposed, in the vicinity of Spruce Street, and relied upon this spring for his water, he must have found plenty of exercise in toting his daily supply from what was the remotest corner of his back yard. There is abundant evidence to prove that springs abounded on the sides of Beacon Hill. A good many years ago, but within the memory of people now living on the Hill, one of these fountains burst forth in the cellar of the house at the westerly corner of Chestnut and Spruce Streets, causing the owner considerable expense to divert it to the sewer. It is, indeed, related that the cost of controlling the water was so great that the lady of the house felt constrained to forego the purchase of a bonnet that season. Was this, perchance, Mr. Blaxton's spring, which had supposedly been choked up in the course of years, but at that time reasserting itself?

It has already been stated that Mr. Bowditch thought that Blaxton's orchard was not located on his six-acre homestead lot, but was high up on the ridge of Mount Vernon where Humphrey Davie had his suburban retreat. Perhaps it was because he missed his apples, or because he was tired of lugging his water from Louisburg Square, quite as much as because, as is said, that he was tired of his new neighbors over on the east side of the Hill, that he finally pulled up stakes and moved to Rhode Island about 1634. One Richard Pepys bought him out and built himself a new house.

He sold, in 1655, to Nathaniel Williams, whose widow sold, in 1676, to her son Nathaniel and to Mary Viall. Young Nathaniel bought Mary's share and sold, in 1708–09, to Thomas Bannister, who had previously purchased the East pasture. At that time there was certainly an orchard on the property, though perhaps it was one planted since Blaxton's time, for the deed specified one in addition to a house, barn, and stables. For some time thereafter this property became known as 'Bannister's Gardens.' Bannister senior died not long after his purchase of this lot, and his wife died in 1711, but the property continued in the possession of their sons and a son-in-law until about 1733, when it was mortgaged to Nathaniel Cunningham, who later foreclosed. Copley bought the place from the Cunningham estate in 1769 and, in 1796,[1] sold it to the Mount Vernon Proprietors, the developing syndicate that overturned all the old pasture fences from Joy and Walnut Streets to the river and from Pinckney Street to the Common, substituting in their place those tree-shaded streets that speedily thereafter became the court end of the town.

[1] February, 1796, L. 182, f. 184; April, 1797, L. 191, f. 167.

II

TRIMOUNTAIN'S SUMMITS

NOT infrequently the question is asked: 'Where was the original summit of Beacon Hill, and how much higher was it than the present summit?' Bowditch answered, with some particularity, the first part of the question in Chapter XLV of his 'Gleaner' papers. The exact height of the old summit is not so easily arrived at, for it does not appear to be a matter of official record, but there are enough available facts of a reasonably dependable nature to warrant the hazarding of a close guess. It was probably about sixty feet higher than the present elevation of its site, which is quite a distance from the present highest point of the Hill, and about fourteen feet lower. The summit elevation to-day is on Mount Vernon Street, a little west of Joy Street, or on the crest of the old-time ridge which connected Beacon Hill and Mount Vernon; in other words, just about where the old Davie's Lane ended at the Humphrey Davie orchard lot.

Since Bowditch's day great changes have come to pass in the appearance of things just east and north of the State House. At that time Mount Vernon Street began at Beacon Street and ran north along the east side of the Bulfinch front and then turned west near the present archway. Temple Street opened out of Mount Vernon Street opposite what was then the northeast corner of the State House. There was a block of houses along the easterly side of Temple Street, while on the west side there was but a single house lot, fronting on Mount Vernon Street, that reached about a third of the way down toward Derne Street. The lower two thirds of that west side block was occupied by the city reservoir. The site of the old town plot of six rods square on the summit of the Hill lay across Temple Street, lapped over a little way into the house and the reservoir on the west, and covered the full depth of the houses opposite. Naturally Mr. Bowditch used these various landmarks in describing the situation of the ancient reservation and the monument that stood in its center, but his words are meaningless to-day unless one resorts to a street plan of that period.

On the plan of the ancient pastures an attempt has been made to adapt his description to the conditions of 1925. The lines of the old town plot and of Sentry Street leading to it from the Common are there shown. The basis of this interpretation is a plan of the State House lot made in 1795 by Osgood Carleton, recorded with Suffolk Deeds (L. 828, f. 266), and three plots by Bowditch illustrating the manner in which the land between Bowdoin Street and the State House was developed for building sites. These plots are found in his original title abstracts (vol. 1, p. 235). These data were carefully plotted upon a plan showing conditions as they were at the time when Bowditch wrote his description in 1855, and the resulting lines were then transferred to a plan of the modern lay-out upon which there remained a sufficient number of unchanged lines to furnish checks and ties. The result does not tally in all respects with the description in the 'Gleaner' article, but Bowditch was there speaking in general terms, whereas the plan is based upon contemporary surveys. The present monument is believed to stand just east of the easterly boundary of the plot. The site of the beacon and that of the original monument is probably at the top of the northerly flight of stone steps leading to the east portico of the State House extension. If this point could be determined instrumentally, it would be historically interesting to mark the site. Surely a landmark founded upon an act of the General Court of the colony in 1634–35, and around which so many interesting incidents in the town's history centered through nearly two centuries, is worthy of such further recognition. Incidentally it is of interest to note that, according to the Street Commissioners' Record of Streets, Sentry Street, as shown upon the accompanying plan, was laid out by the town, March 31, 1640, five years after the erection of the beacon was ordered. The town's title to the summit is recognized in a deed of 1670, quoted by Bowditch, in which a piece of adjacent land is described as 'bordering also on the highway going up to the top of the hill, on the top of which hill lyeth a parcel of land belonging to the town of Boston, i.e., 6 rods square.'

The original monument of stuccoed brick on the site of the old beacon, of which the existing one is a reproduction in stone, was erected in 1790 from designs by Charles Bulfinch, the cost being met by public subscriptions. It stood until 1811, thirteen years after the dedication of the State House, in which year the town, like many of its most substantial citizens, felt the financial pinch of adverse times, and decided to realize on some of its less useful assets, and sold the six-rod plot for ninety-three hundred dollars. The monument fell at that time, for the new owners at once set a gang at work digging down the cone of the hill and carting away the gravel. It seems probable that this work was begun the previous autumn, for in a letter written by Charles Bulfinch's mother to her brother in London, under date of October, 1810, it was stated that 'They are now actually employed in leveling Beacon Hill.'

The not unfamiliar picture of that undertaking, reproduced herewith, is from one of a series of five drawings made at the time by J. R. Smith, an

BEACON HILL AND THE MOUNT VERNON STREET SIDE OF THE ORIGINAL
STATE HOUSE

From a drawing of about 1810

The chimneys of Thurston's house are seen behind the monument, and the spire of Park Street
Church appears to the left of the State House

English drawing-master, who came to Boston about 1808, chromo-lithographs of which were made in 1855 by George G. Smith, a Boston steel engraver.

This was not the first time that the gravel of the cone had been dug into, however, for in 1764 a man named Thomas Hodson, who owned a parcel of land on the Derne Street side, used it as a gravel bank, the excavated material being sold for filling up various low places downtown. The people of the town were much exercised at this defacement of their hill, and a committee of prominent men was appointed to confer with Mr. Hodson, evidently with a view to buying him out. He proved obdurate, however, and the committee recommended that the matter be referred to the Legislature, but no legislation resulted and the digging continued. Many were the laments over the action of the town in selling the hill and thus permitting it to be destroyed, and for many years thereafter the town fathers of that day were execrated as unpatriotic, materialistic vandals. It is doubtful if any one of judgment could be found in the present day who would sympathize with that point of view. Had the hill not fallen at that period, public necessity and convenience would unquestionably have caused its removal later, and long ere this.

Mount Vernon, the westerly summit of Trimountain, had already been cut away and Charles Street raised with its ruins. That, Bowditch states, was in 1804, adding that 'The first railroad ever used in this country was here employed, an inclined plane being laid, down which dirt cars were made to slide, emptying their loads in the water at the foot of the hill.' In a legal memorandum drawn up by H. G. Otis (Otis Papers) in connection with the suit of the Overseers of the Poor, it is stated that 'In 1803 we began our great operation . . . carting down gravel from the mountains.' Dr. Caleb Hopkins Snow, in his 'History of Boston' (1825), stated that the highest point of the west summit was probably between Mount Vernon and Pinckney Streets, and that the west side 'appears to have been rough and precipitous.' The final grading of the northwest slope, along Revere Street, did not come about until the mayoralty of Harrison Gray Otis in 1829. Cotton Hill, the easterly summit, was shaved off in 1835 when Patrick Jackson bought the Gardiner Greene and neighboring estates and developed Pemberton Square as a desirable residential section. In that interesting autobiography of Asa G. Sheldon, already mentioned, he tells how this work was done with one hundred and ninety pick-and-shovel men, and sixty yoke of oxen. His contract price for the excavation was twenty-eight cents a cubic yard. The material was hauled to north of Causeway Street and made eight acres of new land in the old mill pond. Laborers received eighty-three cents a day at the beginning, and this wage was later increased to $1.17. Teamsters, all of them experienced ox-drivers from the country, were paid twenty-six dollars a month and board. The total cost of cutting down the hill and grading the land was something above thirty thousand dollars. The contract called for the completion of the work in six months, but for a bonus of one thousand dollars Sheldon rushed it through in five. When his books were balanced, he found that he had made a profit of about twenty-seven hundred dollars. The maximum cut there was sixty-five feet, and when they reached a depth of fifty-five feet, about in the middle of the present square, they encountered a pocket of what appeared to be marsh mud, about fifteen feet deep. The present-day elevation of Pemberton Square is given as sixty-seven feet above the city base, the official datum which is 7.68 inches below mean low tide. In the days of its old-time glory Cotton Hill was, therefore, one hundred and thirty-two feet above city base.

Such information as has come down to us from early days as to the former height of Beacon Hill is confusingly contradictory. Its highest point to-day is close to one hundred and seven feet above city base, but this point, as previously stated, is about six hundred feet west of the beacon site. At the foot of the existing monument the official elevation is given by the Street Department as 92.7 feet.

This is on the grass within the monument enclosure. The nearest approach to an official record of the height of the old hilltop is found in connection with the celebrated damage suit brought by an abutter whose house was undermined when the hill was dug away. This is found in the twelfth volume of Massachusetts Reports of Supreme Court cases, page 220. There it is stated that the main digging was carried sixty feet below the 'ancient surface of the said next adjoining land,' which was the town lot. Merely adding sixty feet to the present elevation of 92.7 does not furnish an absolutely conclusive solution of the problem, however, for it is not known how much if any was removed at some later time below that first sixty feet testified to in court. Assuming that sixty feet was the most that ever was removed above the present level, then the 'ancient surface' stood at 152.7 feet above city base.

Unhappily for our peace of mind, though, the statement was made in the year 1800, eleven years before the Hill was dug down, that 'The hill rises 138 feet and 6 inches above the level of the sea.' This information is found in a communication by the Reverend John Lathrop, D.D., of Boston, to the American Academy of Arts and Sciences, which was printed as Chapter VIII of Volume III of its 'Memoirs.' He was writing of the springs and wells on the peninsula of Boston in an attempt to ac-

count for the manner in which they were supplied.
It has already been stated that springs abounded
on the sides of the Hill, and that they not infrequently caused householders annoyance by inop-
portunely breaking out in the cellars. Before the
coming of Cochituate water in 1848, every one had
to depend upon a well. These varied in depth, according to Dr. Lathrop, from fifteen or twenty
feet to one hundred or one hundred and twenty
feet, and from a study of the stratification beneath
the city and the surrounding country, he reasoned
that the subterranean waters flowed from various
inland ponds toward the sea, some breaking out on
the surface as springs, others being tapped by wells.
His paper was accompanied by a theoretical dia-
gram illustrating his point.

Even the State House had to have a well in those
days. Dr. Lathrop wrote that it was 'lately dug on
the southeasterly side of Beacon Hill.' While no
definite records remain as to its exact location, it is
readily inferred from certain statutes of that period
providing for fire protective appliances that it was
in the yard at the rear of the Bulfinch front, or, in
other words, between that building and the line
of Mount Vernon Street. Its site was covered by
the Bryant addition in 1853-55. The accompanying picture of the digging is from that side, and it
will be noticed that the excavation had not then
quite reached the level of Mount Vernon Street.

Dr. Lathrop further stated that 'this well is opened at the side of the hill, at a level of about thirty-five feet from the top of the hill, and is ninety-six feet deep.' Continuing, he wrote that 'the hill rises 138 feet and 6 inches above the level of the sea which surrounds the peninsula. The bottom of the well is therefore seven feet and six inches above the level of the sea.'

No authority is cited by him in connection with these figures, but he goes on to state that he had become interested in reports to the effect that the water level within the well varied from time to time, and that he had personally made careful observations of this phenomenon, from which it was clear that the fluctuations were due to the ebb and flow of the sea tides. His studies of these conditions were made in the fall of 1797 and the summer of 1798. On October 10, 1797, at low tide he sounded the well and found that it then contained seven feet eleven inches of water. On the following day at high tide he repeated the operation, and discovered that it was exactly a foot deeper. Although he does not so state, it is naturally inferred that there was an average tide on that occasion, and this assumption is confirmed by the fact that he deliberately chose July 12, 1798, as a day for another observation, because it was the day before the change of the moon, when an unusually high tide might be expected. The result of that sound-

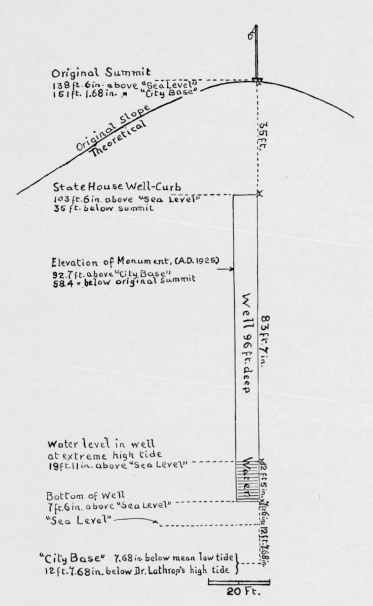

Original Summit
138 ft. 6 in. above "Sea Level"
151 ft. 1.68 in. " "City Base"

Original Slope
Theoretical

State House Well-Curb
103 ft. 6 in. above "Sea Level"
35 ft. below summit

35 ft.

Elevation of Monument, (A.D. 1925)
92.7 ft. above "City Base"
58.4 " below original summit

Well 96 ft. deep

83 ft. 7 in.

Water level in well
at extreme high tide
19 ft. 11 in. above "Sea Level"

Water

12 ft. 5 in. 1 (49.in) 12 ft. 7.68 in.

Bottom of Well
7 ft. 6 in. above "Sea Level"

"Sea Level"

"City Base" 7.68 in. below mean low tide}
12 ft. 7.68 in. below Dr. Lathrop's high tide }

20 Ft.

A CALCULATION OF THE ORIGINAL SUMMIT ELEVATION

Based on Dr. Lathrop's Well Soundings of 1797

ing gave him twelve feet five inches of water in the well, or three feet six inches more than at high tide on the former occasion. His low-tide sounding on the second trial was not made until about an hour and a half after the tide had begun to come in, when he found eleven feet nine inches in the well, or three feet and ten inches more than at the previous dead low water. Then he adds that 'as the bottom of the well is seven feet and six inches above the level of the sea, and the water is found to rise twelve feet and five inches, its elevation may be about twenty feet above the level of the sea.'

Thus he furnished a series of factors for an interesting little calculation in altitude as applied to the summit of the Hill. Working it backward from his 'level of the sea,' we start with seven feet six inches up to the bottom of the well, and then add the twelve feet five inches up to the surface of the water. Of the ninety-six feet of tube, eighty-three feet seven inches remain between the water surface and the well curb. Add that, and the thirty-five feet which he said was the height of the hill-top above the well, and the total is, as he stated, a hundred and thirty-eight feet six inches, or 14.2 feet lower than was arrived at by adding the court record of a sixty-foot cut to the present official elevation at the monument. The discrepancy probably lies between what Dr. Lathrop termed 'the level of the sea' and the 'city base' of to-day, which was not established until some fifty years after his paper was written. What did he mean by the phrase 'the level of the sea'? Did he refer to high water, low water, or mean tide level? The question has been asked of several of the best-informed surveyors in the city, men long identified with public works, and who are themselves interested in antiquarian problems of this nature. They do not know. 'Sea level' does not appear to have had any generally recognized engineering value in those days. After considering his statements as a whole there is an inclination to assume that he referred to the highest tide observed by him, when he stated that the water surface in the well 'may be about twenty feet above the level of the sea.' That tide gave him three feet six inches more water than usual in the well, so that it is concluded that it was not short of a twelve-foot tide in the harbor, which is not phenomenally high, the city records showing many occasions when it has risen fourteen or even fifteen feet. If his 'level of the sea' was the top of that high water, then it is permissible to add 12 feet 7.68 inches to his figure for the height of the Hill in order to harmonize it with elevations founded upon the modern city base. That would bring his summit level up to 151 feet 1.68 inches, or to within a foot and a half of the other result arrived at by adding the court record of a sixty-foot cut to the present elevation of 92.7 feet at the monument.

To be sure, his statement that the top of the Hill rose about thirty-five feet above the point where the well was opened is difficult to reconcile with the conclusion, based upon the court record, that the cone was cut sixty feet to the level of the State House. The only explanation of this discrepancy is through the possibility that the well-curb was at a point higher than the State House foundations. It is not improbable that the well was dug about as soon as the construction was started on the building, in order to supply water for the operation, and that was sixteen years before the 'great digging' began.

Both Dr. Snow in his 'History,' of 1825, already referred to, and Dr. N. B. Shurtleff in his 'History,' published by the city in 1870, adopt the summit elevation figure of 138.5 feet, but neither cites his authority. It is a fair presumption that they accepted Lathrop's statement and did not question his sea-level datum. William W. Wheildon, in his admirable monograph on the Hill of 1877, frankly quotes Lathrop, but offers no comment.

Another check upon the variation between the official city elevation figures of one hundred years ago and now is found in an old plan on file in the Street Laying-Out Department at City Hall (Plan Book No. 1, p. 3). This plan covers both sides of

Mount Vernon Street from Joy to just west of Walnut Street. It is not dated, but from the fact that it shows the locations of the houses existing at the time when it was made, it seems clear that it represents conditions not later than early in 1822. Four houses built on the south side of Mount Vernon Street in that year are not shown. This plan is of interest in the present connection because of the elevation figures that it bears. One of the stations is at the edge of the property line on the north side of Mount Vernon Street opposite the head of Walnut, in front of Numbers 59 and 61. That elevation is given as 91.8 feet. Comparing this with a Street Department elevation of 1920, taken on the curbstone opposite Walnut Street, which was 102.78 feet, shows a difference of .02 of a foot short of eleven feet, which is not accounted for by any radical change of grade at that point in the past hundred years. What their datum was is not known. Probably it was not the same as Dr. Lathrop's 'sea level.' Certainly it was not the present 'city base,' which was not established for at least thirty years after that old plan was made. It serves, however, to indicate the reasonableness of the assumption that the old summit of Beacon Hill was ten feet or more higher than has been hitherto given.

The probability is that the court figures are as close to correct as will ever be known, and if they are accepted, then any one who is desirous of satisfying his eye as to the ancient natural surface level may simply walk across the little park opposite Ashburton Place and look up to the bronze eagle perched at the top of the sixty-foot monument.

III

SOCIAL TRANSITIONS OF A CENTURY

SOME one in a whimsical mood once defined the social-geographic distinction between the south and the north slopes of the Hill as the 'nabob' and the 'bob' sides. To determine the exact line of demarcation between the two at any time within half a century or more, it has only been necessary to consult the Boston Blue Book. Anything north of Pinckney Street, except perhaps Charles Street, was always beyond the social pale, and notwithstanding that here and there throughout that section there lived people of some distinction, and many of entire respectability. The northeast quadrant east of Joy Street managed to hold its head high for many years. Charles Sumner, during his senatorship, lived at 20 Hancock Street, and men of mark in many lines had their homes on Temple, Bowdoin and adjacent streets.

But that section north of Pinckney Street from Joy Street to the river, and again excepting Charles Street after that had been developed, never enjoyed the favor of the socially elect. Portions of that area were the scene of the earliest attempts at real estate developments. That was in the younger years of the eighteenth century. Judging from the somewhat restrained allusions to that neighborhood by contemporary writers and antiquaries, it is concluded that its original population was not of a high order. Indeed, it seems to have required many years, and a change of street names in some instances, to overcome the prejudice against that vicinity held by respectable members of the community. Shortly before the opening of the nineteenth century, a change came over that northwest slope and a village of detached and semi-detached houses, many of them of wood, grew up, the homes of prosperous mechanics and tradesmen in the main, with a sprinkling of seafaring men and laborers.

After the Revolution a number of families of freed negroes established themselves in some of the older and cheaper houses of that section, and gradually, street by street, came to possess it in large measure, until, as a result, that entire slope lost its association with Beacon Hill in the popular mind and acquired a sobriquet of its own. By the end of another century the neighborhood began to show signs of a new transformation. The older wooden houses, and not a few of the brick ones as well, many sadly fallen to decay, began to disappear before an energetic programme of low-priced apartment-house construction.

Meantime, during a hundred years or a trifle more, the southwest slope, from the crest of old Mount Vernon to the Common and the water, had developed under the administration of a group

of sagacious owners and their children into a little
town by itself, peopled in the main by families of
affluence and social prominence. Until the building of the new State House in 1795, Beacon Street
had seemed to Bostonians a relatively remote
suburb. Nor did the wealthy begin to look covet-
ously toward a residence on the Hill until Senator
Mason and Squire Otis had themselves built mansions upon the ridge. That was not until 1802, or
six years after the Mount Vernon Proprietors inserted their first advertisement in the 'Columbian
Centinel'[1] which proclaimed that 'Divers House
Lots, in Copeley's and Allen's Pastures so-called,'
were for sale. Because of the quaintness of phrase,
and because the vision of the Proprietors is there
in a measure revealed, it is interesting to read on in
that three inches of display advertisement that
'The public are invited to turn their attention
to these Lands, which afford the best situations
in town. . . . The varied fall of these Lands, is
adapted to the circumstances of those who wish
merely for genteel and airy situations, and of those
who would unite to their advantages the convenience of Boarding Houses, and accommodations for
business. Their proximity to the new State House,
renders it convenient for those who are desirous
of accommodating the Members of the General
Court. . . .'

[1] Issue of August 3, 1796.

MRS. JONATHAN MASON
By Gilbert Stuart

SOCIAL TRANSITIONS OF A CENTURY

There was a period, not so many years back, when it seemed as if that reference to boarding-houses was prophetic, and that this business was destined to possess the Hill on every side. It is evident, however, that the original syndicate had no intention of promoting that type of habitation except perhaps on the Pinckney Street side. Nor did they foresee the probability that business offices and stores would ever encroach on the Beacon Street frontage. The allusion in the advertisement to possible commercial locations referred to the river front, and perhaps to Charles Street, though the latter developed early as a residence street, save for an occasional market, grocery, or drug store.

In the several chapters dealing with the details of the upbuilding of that southerly side, it is shown how the varying economic conditions of the country were reflected in this enterprise. The project was launched in a period of astonishing material prosperity, and during a time when the population of the city was increasing phenomenally, which naturally led to a house shortage. Just as this land began to move in the market, the slump due to the Federal Embargo against foreign trade set in, followed by the depression of war in 1812. High-tariff advocates point to the fact that the virtual free-trade legislation following the war caused a continuance of widespread business distress. They likwise claim that the renewal of prosperity in 1824 was the result of the readoption of the protective-tariff policy. The Hill certainly suffered neglect during the war and until the early twenties, and some of its wealthy residents were among those financially prostrated.

Then came another burst of building, greater in volume than before, but more modest in style, and this in turn was checked by the panic of 1829 which carried ruin for many in its wake, among them some of the residents and builders on the Hill. Early in the thirties building was renewed only to be brought again to a standstill by yet another panic in 1837, which the tariff advocates also attribute to a free-trade movement. By that time the available house sites of the fashionable quarter had been largely occupied, and there were few additions until the late forties and early fifties when some of the original houses were replaced by more costly structures.

In the early days of the Hill's fashionable development, when life was more formal than now, the grandees of Boston are supposed to have been much on their dignity, in all public places at least. It is somewhat surprising, therefore, to read, in a little book of reminiscences, written forty-odd years ago [1] that in the author's boyhood, between

[1] *Old Boston Town Early in this Century.* 'By An 1801-er' (James W. Hale, of New York). 1880.

1805 and 1825, 'Almost any morning might be seen Colonel Thomas H. Perkins, Harrison Gray Otis, William (Billy) Gray, Ben Bussey, Peter C. Brooks, Israel Thorndike and other wealthy folk, trudging homeward for their eight o'clock breakfast, with their market baskets containing their one o'clock dinner.' If that anecdote can be trusted as historically correct, there was no lack of honest democracy concealed beneath the prim clothes of that period.

Then there came a period when the houses of the Hill began to be regarded as 'old-fashioned,' a term which then implied something short of admiration for anything savoring of the antique. The 'new land' of the Back Bay, with its broad and sunnier streets, proved an irresistible magnet to many. Gradually, through the sixties and seventies, the exodus progressed until Mount Vernon and Chestnut and the adjoining streets were bereft of many family names that had become familiar through two generations of residence. Tradition, and an appreciation of the Hill's natural advantages, held a family here and there despite the pull of fashion and the encroachment of the boarding-house.

With the turn of the century, however, another change set in. The Hill began to be rediscovered as a desirable place of residence. Old houses, both large and small, were refitted, and family names,

47

long strangers to the neighborhood, once more appeared, represented this time by a younger generation. In time even boarding-houses dwindled in number, giving way to quarters for the kitchen-ette housekeepers. Wherever there remained a good old house, however seedy and down at the heel, and quite regardless of its immediate environ-ment, an enthusiastic reclaimer brought it back to its old or even better estate. Thus the nabob south slope was recaptured, and the invading army swarmed across the ridge and began descending the northerly side. And so the Hill returned to its own.

IV

THE MOUNT VERNON PROPRIETORS

OF the houses on the southwest side of Beacon Hill, built before the syndicate known as the Mount Vernon Proprietors began their wholesale development of that slope by buying the Copley and other properties in 1795, none remains. The last one to disappear was the Hancock house, built about 1735, and torn down in 1863. Those older houses were not numerous. Along Beacon Street, between Somerset Street and the old water front, which was just east of Charles Street, there were eight houses, all but one of pre-Revolutionary date. Close to the westerly corner of Somerset Street was the residence of Edward Bromfield, whose next-door neighbor on the west was the Honorable James Bowdoin, one of the early governors of the Commonwealth, and the suppressor of Shays's Rebellion. Those houses, both frame structures of manorial proportions, occupied commanding positions on the slope of the ridge which then connected Beacon and Cotton Hills, or in the rear of the present School Committee building and the Hotel Bellevue. This ridge was cut away in 1845 as a final operation in the transformation of the Hill's topography, and these old houses disappeared.' Where the East Wing of the

State House now stands was the mansion of William Molineaux, one of the distinguished patriots of the town. West of the State House was the Hancock house, with its grounds extending over the hill almost to Derne Street and as far west as Joy Street.

Below Joy Street were four wooden houses. That street took its name from Dr. John Joy, an apothecary, who bought the two acres now bounded by Joy, Beacon, Walnut, and Mount Vernon Streets, and built a house on the site of the Tudor Apartments in 1791. It remained until 1833, when it was taken down and again set up at South Boston. Just below Walnut Street were three houses which had belonged to John Singleton Copley, the painter, and in one of which he lived until his departure for England just prior to the Revolution. The location of the two upper houses of this group is readily placed, with the aid of Withington's plan of 1796,[1] on which they are shown, and by the very definite deed descriptions of the two lots at the time when they changed hands in 1816 and 1818.[2] They are also shown on a plan of the city drawn by John Groves Hales in 1814, a portion of which, covering the Hill, is here reproduced. The site of the third house is sufficiently well fixed by the recorded testimony of several citizens who remembered the building.

[1] L. 192, f. 198.
[2] L. 252, f. 69, 70; L. 259, f. 193; L. 263, f. 90; L. 268, f. 86.

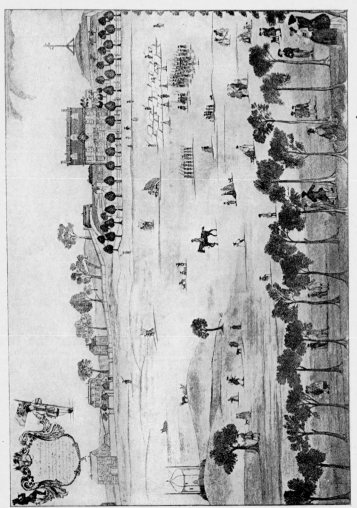

'A PROSPECTIVE VIEW OF PART OF THE COMMONS'

From a water-color drawing by Christian Remick in 1768

These depositions [1] were taken in 1810 and in 1836 in connection with two lawsuits brought against the Proprietors to oust them from certain portions of the land claimed under Copley's deed. The earlier suit was brought by heirs of Nathaniel Cunningham, the other by the Overseers of the Poor.[2] All three of the Copley houses are shown in a water-color drawing made by Christian Remick in 1768, entitled 'A Prospective [sic] View of Part of the Commons,' and now owned by the Concord Antiquarian Society.

The house nearest Walnut Street (39 and 40 Beacon Street) the Proprietors sold in 1796 to Charles Cushing, Clerk of the Supreme Court, and the house next west (41 and 42 Beacon Street) was bought at the same time by John Vinal, school-master, and later Justice of the Peace. As will be seen shortly, Mr. Vinal had previously lived for many years in the Cushing house. The westerly of the three Copley houses was probably built prior to 1694, in which year the Francis East pasture, in the southeast corner of which it stood, was sold, with a house then on it, to Thomas Bannister. Several of the recorded depositions referred to above mention this old house as having been long inhabited by a man named Ephraim Fenno,

---

[1] L. 221, f. 107, 230, 231, 252, 272; L. 382, f. 265; L. 387, f. 247, 253; L. 413, f. 19; L. 436, f. 130.
[2] Otis Papers, and 'Gleaner.'

a leather-dresser by trade, but who there sold 'cakes and ale.' There was also an old barn (so designated by Vinal and Cushing in their depositions) that stood for many years between the Fenno house and what is now Spruce Street. According to a deposition made by Catherine Searl in 1810 (L. 221, f. 250), when she was eighty-eight years old, Fenno was a tenant there when the East place was owned by Nathaniel Cunningham, of Brighton. The witness was a member of the Cunningham household in those days and recalled that the owner regarded Fenno as 'a worthless fellow.' Vinal said that his children were well educated.

No direct and convincing evidence has been found to indicate in which of his houses Copley himself lived. Drake, in his 'Landmarks' (p. 334), states that the Somerset Club is on the site of his home. The middle one of his three houses stood there. Other antiquarian students have been of the opinion that Copley lived in the easterly house, the site of 39 and 40 Beacon Street. A careful study of all the deeds covering these properties, the depositions of Vinal, Charles Cushing, Jr., Robert Treat Paine, and Joseph Moncrief, the statements of 'Gleaner' and Drake, the tax records of the town from 1780 (the earliest extant) to 1797, the United States tax on dwellings of 1798, the recorded plan of Copley's property made for the Proprietors in

1796, and on which the two easterly houses are shown, the water-color of 1768 already referred to, and Hales's property map of 1814, seem to confirm Drake in his statement that Copley lived on the Somerset Club site.

Copley did not begin buying his Beacon Hill land until 1769. Fenno was then a tenant in the old house — had been, in fact, for some twenty years — and continued there through 1785 at least, as the tax records show. Vinal was authority for the statement that Copley's mother, Mrs. Peter Pelham, who acted as agent for her son during his absence in England, put Fenno out and had the house demolished. This must have been before 1789 in which year Mrs. Pelham died, and was probably three years earlier. Vinal himself lived in both of the upper houses at various times. By his recorded testimony it is shown that he rented the easterly house from 1760 to 1764, which was before Copley bought the property, and again, in 1781, after an absence of seventeen years from Boston, he returned to the same house which he then hired of Mrs. Pelham. In the course of his deposition Vinal stated that he 'then was informed that he [Copley] was the owner, not only of that house, but the next.' Silvester Gardiner, an apothecary on Marlborough (Washington) Street, had bought the Vinal lot in 1746 (L. 73, f. 6) and the Cushing lot in 1751 (L. 80, f. 95), the latter having a house upon it at the time. When Copley bought these two lots of Gardiner in 1770 (L. 117, f. 129), two houses were included from which it is inferred that Gardiner built the one on the Vinal lot at some time subsequent to 1746.

In the first Boston Directory, published in 1789, Vinal is given as living in the 'first house below Gov. Hancock,' which would be the site of 39 and 40 Beacon Street. There is nothing in Vinal's testimony to show that he moved to the middle house (41 and 42 Beacon Street) before he purchased it of the Proprietors in 1796, and the tax records between 1788 and 1796 do not clearly indicate which house he occupied during that period, although before and after those dates they are sufficiently specific.

To be sure, Mr. Paine, who had been Copley's counsel in 1769 when the latter bought the Fenno house and land, testified that he well remembered 'Mr. Copley being in possession of the house now occupied by Charles Cushing,' which was the easterly house. But being 'in possession of' is not necessarily the same as 'living in.' No one questions the fact that Copley 'possessed' that house. Joseph Moncrief, who lived on May (Myrtle or Revere) Street in his youth, went on record as remembering Copley, 'who lived in a house by the side of the Common in which Justice Vinal afterward lived.' Here is testimony as to the house in which

54

Copley 'lived,' but inasmuch as Vinal had by that time lived in both houses, no proof is given as to Copley's residence. Moncrief's evidence was given in 1836, his memory running back to just before the Revolution when he was ten or eleven years old. Vinal sold his house to David Sears, Jr., in 1818.

The best test of the question as to which house was Copley's own residence seems to lie in a determination, if possible, of which was the larger and more commodious dwelling, it being assumed that Copley would naturally take for his own occupancy the better one. In the 1768 water-color showing the houses on the Beacon Street frontage, there are three dwellings west of the Hancock house. Although extremely amateurish in its handling, the painter evidently aimed to present a truthful picture within the limits of his ability to draw. The first house below Hancock's is represented as being relatively small and set close to the street, while the house next west of that is much more commodious in appearance, and stands well back in its fenced or walled grounds. A third house, flush with the street, probably Fenno's, is next, while a little below it, at the edge of the drawing, is a portion of another building, very likely the barn which both Vinal and Cushing mentioned in their depositions.

Thirteen years after that drawing was made, Vinal returned to live in the 'first house below

Gov. Hancock,' and he stated that since his earlier tenancy there it had 'undergone some alterations and additions.' No other record evidence as to the relative sizes of these houses is found until 1798, two years after Cushing and Vinal had bought the properties. The Fenno house had then been gone for ten years or more. In that year the houses are roughly described in the records of the United States tax.[1] Both were there entered as wooden dwellings, two stories high. Cushing's house had a ground area of fourteen hundred and forty square feet, had thirty-five windows, and was valued at thirty-five hundred dollars. Vinal's house covered seventeen hundred and twenty square feet of ground, had one less window, and was valued at four thousand dollars. Moreover, as will be seen later, Copley himself stated that the westerly house rented for forty pounds a year more than the other one. Obviously there is nothing conclusive in any of these statements and records, but, after considering all the known facts, there is an irresistible inclination to agree with Drake in the belief that Copley lived on the sites of 41 and 42 Beacon Street.[2]

[1] Twenty-Second Report, Boston Record Commission, pp. 305, 320.
[2] Further testimony as to Copley's own residence is found in an article written by Mrs. E. S. Oakey, a granddaughter of Mrs. Swan, of the Mount Vernon Proprietors, and printed in *Scribner's Monthly* for January, 1881, p. 416 *et seq.* Mrs. Oakey was the daughter of William Sullivan, who married Mrs. Swan's second daughter, to whom her mother gave the house at 15 Chestnut Street in 1807.

THE MOUNT VERNON PROPRIETORS

North of Beacon Street the hill rose rapidly to the main summit behind the State House and to Mount Vernon, the westerly of the three heights of Trimountain, the highest point of which appears to have been just east of Louisburg Square. The Humphrey Davie house, built sometime subsequent to 1665, on the orchard lot just west of Joy Street on Mount Vernon, seems to have disappeared before the Mount Vernon Proprietors began their operations. Other buildings then existing on the lands purchased by them appear on their plans (L. 192, f. 198), but this particular lot is shown as vacant pasture. The Hill in those days 'was exactly like the country, with trees, bushes, shrubs, and flowers.' At least it was so described by Joseph Moncrief in his deposition. He had rambled over the Hill as a boy and knew it intimately. On the northwest slope of the Hill, streets had been laid out as early as 1730, and a number of small and scattered houses had been built between Myrtle and Cambridge Streets. On the southerly

Mrs. Oakey wrote that she was born in that house in 1810 and that she lived there throughout her girlhood. From this house she could look out 'over a low wooden house, surrounded by a garden,' to the Common. There were no houses on the opposite side of Chestnut Street until 1823. Continuing, Mrs. Oakey wrote, speaking of the 'low wooden house,' that 'In this house John Singleton Copley, the artist, had lived, and in it his son, afterward Lord Lyndhurst, was born. This house was occupied later by General Knox, and, at the time of which I write, by Judge Vinal. Mr. David Sears once owned the place and built upon it a house for himself, and, later, two for his daughters.'

side of Myrtle Street were three ropewalks reaching from near Hancock Street to below Grove Street, and the back yards of the present-day houses on the north side of Pinckney Street abut upon what was formerly the ropewalk property. A tar house connected with one of these ropewalks was located south of that line, or on the rear of the lots now numbered 41 and 43 Pinckney Street. There were other ropewalks along the easterly side of Hancock Street on land now within the State House extension enclosure.

Bowditch, in his 'Gleaner' papers, named the members of the syndicate known as the Mount Vernon Proprietors and their respective interests in the enterprise of developing the Hill as follows: 'Jonathan Mason and H. G. Otis, each three-tenths, and Benjamin Joy two-tenths; while the remaining two-tenths were held by General Henry Jackson, and more recently by Wm. Sullivan, as trustees of Hepsibah Swan, wife of James Swan, and subject to her appointment.' It is quite evident, however, from certain letters and other documents found among the Papers of Mr. Otis, and from one of Bulfinch's depositions (L. 387, f. 253; L. 413, f. 19), that Mr. Joy and Mrs. Swan were not charter members, so to speak, of the syndicate, but that they bought out some of the original subscribers soon after the launching of the enterprise. Among the Otis Papers there is a letter,

CHARLES BULFINCH

MRS. JAMES SWAN

HARRISON GRAY OTIS

JONATHAN MASON

FOUR OF THE MOUNT VERNON PROPRIETORS

dated at Boston June 17, 1795, addressed to Captain James Scott, relative to the negotiations then under way for the purchase of Copley's land. This letter is signed by all of the then members of the syndicate and in this order, William Scollay, Charles Bulfinch, Jonathan Mason, Jr., Joseph Woodward, Harrison Gray Otis. Scollay was a retired apothecary and Woodward was a merchant. Captain Scott was master of a ship owned by John Hancock, and as he was a capable and dependable person, whose voyages took him frequently to London, the Proprietors retained him to carry on the negotiations with Copley. The above-mentioned letter confirms this fact of Scott's connection with the transaction, for it opens with a reference to his having been entrusted, on a previous voyage, with a commission to secure a sale agreement from Copley. It then requests Scott, on his arrival in London, to tender the cash, in the sum agreed upon, to Copley, and to demand that he execute the deed, which was also enclosed, to Scott.

There is also among the Otis Papers an extended memorandum entitled 'Defendants' Title,' written by Mr. Otis in 1837 in connection with the Overseers' suit, which is in fact an outline history of the entire Mount Vernon undertaking from 1794 to the date of the document. Mr. Otis did not there name all his partners, but he did state that Charles Bulfinch was 'one of the then Proprietors' in 1796.

Bulfinch himself told the story completely when he was put upon the stand as a witness in that same suit, and the deposition, which formed an important part of his testimony, is of record in Suffolk Deeds. He there stated that at the time of the Copley purchase the Proprietors were Jonathan Mason, Harrison Gray Otis, Joseph Woodward, William Scollay, and himself, each owning a fifth interest.

Bulfinch sold out to Benjamin Joy in 1797, or just about a year after the purchase from Copley had been finally consummated. The Woodward and Scollay interests were purchased by Mason, Otis, and the trustee for Mrs. Swan. Later, in 1799, Mason and Otis deeded to Joy a one-fifth interest in the entire property (L. 192, f. 184). Mr. Bulfinch's withdrawal was probably due to financial difficulties connected with the building of the Tontine Crescent block in Franklin Place, in which enterprise he was a partner. Mr. Joy was perhaps prompted to go to his relief by the fact that Mrs. Joy was a daughter of Mr. Joseph Barrell, in whose mercantile office Mr. Bulfinch served an apprenticeship after his graduation at Harvard, and before he decided upon architecture as a profession. It is known that Mr. Barrell took a great interest in the young man, and that the families were intimate.

V

COPLEY TITLE COMPLEXITIES

AFTER purchasing the Copley and Allen lands, the partners proceeded to square out their domain on the northeast by purchasing from the heirs of Enoch Brown a piece of the old Bosworth pasture which lay along the north side of Mount Vernon Street, from opposite the head of Walnut Street east to Joy Street, and north to the ropewalks. In that particular transaction Daniel Staniford and Joseph Carnes, the latter one of the ropewalk owners, were partners, although they were not named in the conveyances.[1] This gave them a continuous east-and-west line from Joy Street to the river. Later they bought the remainder of the Phillips pasture north to Cambridge Street.

The development of Mount Vernon was undoubtedly the most important real estate enterprise until then ever undertaken in Boston. For some time previously there had been a wave of exceptional prosperity whereby old fortunes had expanded and new ones had been created. The older residential sections of the town were, therefore, no longer able to afford sufficient sites for fine

[1] Bowditch Abstracts, vol. 8, p. 46.

houses. On the commanding heights of Mount Vernon, overlooking the Common on the one hand, and the broad expanse of the Charles River and the Brookline hills beyond on the other, there was ample room for the development of a court end of high distinction. That the enterprise proved an expensive undertaking, and that there was not as great a rush for house lots as had apparently been anticipated, is shown by the statement in that 'memorandum' of 1837 by Mr. Otis, already referred to, that the first cost to the Proprietors was more than forty thousand dollars, 'the sales slow and far between.' Those first costs probably represented the purchase of the Copley, Allen, and Brown lands, legal fees incurred in Boston and London in connection with the suit to oblige Copley to abide by the sale agreement executed in his name by his Boston agent, Samuel Cabot (L. 387, f. 253), the three hundred dollars paid to Captain Scott for his services as intermediary in that transaction, interest on money borrowed to meet the Copley purchase, surveying charges, also quit-claim deeds covering fourteen small parcels, enumerated in a memorandum (Otis Papers), lying within the supposed boundaries of Copley and Allen to which others laid claim. The Proprietors made every effort to safeguard their title through settlement with claimants, and, as Mr. Otis afterward wrote in a brief (Otis Papers), they paid three or four times over for portions of the land. Among the Otis Papers there are numerous references to these transactions, the most interesting of all being a rough draft of an accounting of money paid in connection with the Copley deal. For the eleven acres of upland and the adjacent river flats, amounting to about nine acres additional, the Proprietors agreed to pay Copley three thousand guineas, English money, which, at the then prevailing exchange, amounted to fourteen thousand dollars. The accounting statement referred to contains the entry: 'Money finally paid for Copeley [*sic*] purchase, £5350 Sterling.' This the accountant changed into American money farther down and entered a total of $23,777.76, with the notation that 'Of this sum Copeley received $14,000.' The deed price of the Allen eight acres was sixty-one hundred dollars, and of the Brown pasture ten thousand dollars. If to these items is added the various fees and court charges already alluded to, and the cost of the quitclaims, the sum total reaches the 'more than forty thousand dollars' named by Mr. Otis as the first cost of the properties.

It is a well-known fact that Copley repented of his bargain with the Proprietors even before it was finally consummated and endeavored to abrogate it. Bulfinch testified in 1836 (L. 436, f. 130) that 'Copley thought his agent had sold the land for less than its value and refused to execute the deed.'

This led to an action in the Boston courts to enforce the terms of the trade. Eventually Copley's son, himself an English lawyer (later Baron Lyndhurst, Lord Chancellor), came to Boston with power of attorney and completed the transaction according to the original agreement. Among the Otis Papers there are numerous letters, some from Copley to his Boston agent, and other collateral documents bearing on this subject. It appears from these that Copley bought the larger part of the property (from 43 Beacon Street west to the river, flats included) for £120, lawful money, equal perhaps to $400. This was regarded as a bargain price, the Cunningham estate being obliged to sell in order to provide cash with which to meet a demand of the Town of Cambridge for £18 1s. 3d., incurred in the public support of two aged negroes who had belonged to the elder Cunningham. There was also another reason for the apparent cheapness of these lands. An heir of a previous owner, Bannister, had entered a claim to it, and for this reason no warrant of title could be given by Cunningham's administrator. Copley took the risk and was sued, but the court found in Copley's favor. For the two houses bought of Silvester Gardiner, and a pasture running back to the Allen land, Copley paid £650, perhaps equal to $2164, and for a strip the full length of Walnut Street, bought of John Williams, £90, or $300. Thus his entire twenty acres of that they were built by the partners on joint account, probably with a view to stimulating developments in that street which was laid out in 1799. In three separate deeds, identical in form, the earliest dated November 29, 1800, his partners conveyed to Mr. Joy their eight-tenths of this property, which was described as 'a certain piece or parcel of land . . . upon Copeley's [*sic*] Hill or pasture with eight-tenths of the new house erected on said land and the celler and materials remaining of the house lately consumed thereon. The whole of said land is bounded by the new fence on the westerly side, and on the easterly side is to extend from the celler now remaining there 25 feet and to be bounded by a line to be parallel to said celler and 25 feet distant. On the northerly part said land is bounded on Olive Street, and on the southerly side on Chestnut Street, meaning hereby to sell my undivided [stated fractional interest] of said house, celler, and land from Olive to Chestnut Street 25 feet distant each side of said building and celler.'

Except for the statement that this land runs through from Chestnut Street to Mount Vernon, there is nothing in the deeds definitely to fix its boundaries. It is quite apparently located between Walnut and Willow Streets (the latter, unnamed, is referred to in a deed of 1808 from Joy to Jeremiah Gardner, as 'laid out by the Proprietors of Mount Vernon'), for below that point there were no building developments for six or eight years, at which time three houses were built on the opposite side of Chestnut Street below Spruce. From an examination of other deeds, some from Joy covering portions of this property, and some describing adjoining lots, it is possible to locate this land as extending on Chestnut Street from 29A to 37 — that is, from the Theological School Chapel to Willow Street — up that street to Mount Vernon, and easterly on that street to the school property again.

It seems likely that the statement in the deed that the property extended '25 feet distant each side of said building and celler' was erroneous so far as it referred to the western boundary. If that was the correct description, then 'the new fence' previously named in the same deed as the western line must have stood on the party line between 35 and 37 Chestnut Street, the latter abutting on Willow Street on the west. Inasmuch as Mr. Joy owned the site of 37 and sold it in 1824 to be built upon, and since no deed to Joy covering that lot independently has been found, it must be assumed that the fence was actually on the easterly line of Willow Street. Furthermore, the fence is specifically referred to in a deed from Joy to Gardner, 1808, as the western boundary of that portion of this land cornering on Willow and Mount Vernon Streets.

THE PROPRIETORS' EARLIEST VENTURE

The present house at 29A Chestnut Street faces east upon a charming side garden twenty-five feet wide, the easterly boundary of which is the school chapel. It is natural to presume, therefore, that this house was built on the ruins of the one that was burned. The other house must have stood on the site of either 31 or 33 Chestnut Street. If 29A was the house that burned, it seems probable that the other building was detached, otherwise it is hardly likely that it would have escaped destruction also. Since it is known that there were no houses on the sites of 35 and 37 until 1823 and 1824, it is assumed that Number 33, many years ago rebuilt in brown stone, occupies the position of the house that was saved.

Evidently Mr. Joy at once rebuilt on the old cellar and added another house, for in 1802 he was taxed as living there and as owning two unoccupied houses as well. No other houses were assessed that year nearer to him than the two old Copley houses just below Walnut Street on Beacon, and the Mason and Otis mansions on Mount Vernon. Judging from the details of the tax list, and from the fact that in certain mortgages given by Mr. Joy the occupants of the houses were named, it is concluded that Mr. Joy himself lived in Number 33 until about 1810. Until that year his other houses had been rented. In 1803 Nathaniel Lee lived at 29A, and during the next three years General

David Humphreys was a tenant there until his new house, 89 Mount Vernon Street, was completed. In 1808, Ebenezer Rockwood, later a tenant of Jonathan Mason at 57 Mount Vernon Street, occupied that house, but the following year it was sold to Gideon Snow, who seems to have been related to Mrs. Joy. Mr. Snow lived there until he bought a new house on the opposite side of the street about 1817, at which time he sold 29A to Charles R. Codman (L. 255, f. 214), son of the Honorable John Codman, for seven thousand dollars. It seems probable that Mr. Codman made extensive alterations in this house. Judging from the fact that the masonry in the swell front differs from that in the other exposed walls, it is suspected that this feature may have been one of the additions at that time. The purple window glass is a further indication that changes were made then, since these tinted panes are only found elsewhere in houses built between 1818 and 1824.[1] At Number 31 Thomas Perkins seems to have been the first tenant in 1803 and 1804, during which years he was building his own mansion on the corner of Mount Vernon and Joy Streets, as described in another chapter. Stephen Salisbury, Jr., followed Mr. Perkins, and when Mr. Joy sold 29A to Mr. Snow in 1809, the deed stated that the property was bounded on the west by 'a wall which divides the

[1] See Chapter XIX.

THE SWAN HOUSES, 13, 15, AND 17 CHESTNUT STREET, 1806
Probably by Bulfinch. Recessed arch windows on first floor; band course
between first and second stories; full-length windows on second story

FIRST HOUSE BUILT BY THE MOUNT VERNON PRO-
PRIETORS. 29A CHESTNUT STREET. 1799 OR 1800
Once the home of Edwin Booth

The next houses built in Chestnut Street after Mr. Joy took possession of the Willow Street corner were Numbers 6 and 8 on the south side near Walnut Street, and Numbers 27 to 29, the site of the chapel. In June, 1803, Charles Paine, son of Robert Treat Paine, and son-in-law of Charles Cushing, bought the site of Number 6 and 8, and the following year he was assessed for 'two new houses unfinished.' In 1805, the tax record indicates that he was living in one of these, and that the other was unoccupied. Their tax value at the time was six thousand dollars each. In those days these houses had side yards with driveways to the stables in the rear. Twenty years later the property was bought by Cornelius Coolidge who built Numbers 4 and 10 on the yard areas.

In January, 1804, Captain Richard Crowninshield Derby, formerly of Salem, bought the lot now occupied by the Theological School and its chapel. On the Chestnut Street frontage he built a handsome house with stables on the Mount Vernon Street side. He paid four thousand dollars for the land. The following year the tax value of this 'new house' was sixteen thousand dollars, and in 1806 it was raised to twenty-six thousand dollars. Merely from a comparison of the assessed values of this house with those of others in the neighborhood, it is evident that this was an unusually magnificent mansion. Mr. Joy's houses were assessed that year for but eight thousand dollars apiece. Mr. Ogden Codman, grandson of Charles R. Codman, who lived next door at 29A, speaking from his wide architectural knowledge of the older houses of the town, says that this was by all odds the finest house ever built on that street, and that its dining-room, modeled on that of the Petit Trianon at Versailles, was equipped with a movable floor through which the table was lowered to the room below for resetting between courses, the floor automatically closing as the table sank to the lower level.

In referring to the deeds to Mr. Joy, attention was called to the spelling there of the surname 'Copeley.' The same spelling is found in the body of the original deed to the Mount Vernon Proprietors in 1795. It might be inferred from this that the present form, as known to Bostonians in Copley Square, is a corruption, but such is not the case. The grantor's signature to the deed and elsewhere is invariably 'Copley.' The 'Copeley' form is found in many contemporary documents, even in letters and memoranda in the hand of Harrison Gray Otis,[1] as noticed in Chapters IV and V, and this indicates clearly enough that the name was pronounced 'Cope-ley' and not 'Cop-ley' as now. So in the case of Captain Derby, it is repeatedly found that the assessors wrote his name

[1] Otis Papers.

167

on their records as 'Darby,' a phonetic reproduction of the English pronunciation then in vogue here. Similarly what Bostonians to-day call 'Bromfield' was formerly pronounced 'Broomfield' by the members of that family, and there is evidence to show that the Faneuil family name was spoken as 'Funnel.' Bowdoin Street, named for the Governor of that name, was not spoken as 'Bowd'n' in the old days. The writer recalls that in his boyhood certain elderly people always referred to the street and to the college as 'Bowdoh-in,' which itself is a far cry from the original French of the Huguenot ancestor, Pierre Baudouin.

Mrs. Swan, of the Mount Vernon Proprietors, built three houses, now 13, 15, and 17 Chestnut Street, and in 1806 they were assessed to General Henry Jackson, agent, as 'three new houses.' These·houses were given by Mrs. Swan to her three daughters upon their marriage, 13 to Mrs. John Turner Sargent in 1806, 15 to Mrs. William Sullivan in 1807, and 17 to Mrs. John C. Howard in 1808. With these houses went three stables fronting on Mount Vernon Street, now numbered 50, 56, and 60. Despite the apparent gaps in the sequence of these numbers, these stables stood in a row. During the middle and latter part of the last century the two upper stables were occupied by a grocer, an upholsterer, and a provision store. Since the Club of Odd Volumes became the occupant of those buildings, some of the superfluous numbers have been dropped, although there apparently never was a door numbered 58. Number 60 has long been used as a studio by Miss Elizabeth Bartol, the occupant of 17 Chestnut Street, and a great-granddaughter of Mrs. Swan.

These one-story brick buildings invariably attract the attention of the stranger, who not unnaturally wonders at what seems to be a singularly wasteful use of valuable land. Mrs. Swan's deeds to her daughters are entirely responsible for this situation, for they provided in each case that 'the roof of the said stable shall never be raised more than thirteen feet above Olive Street.' Another provision of these deeds requires the perpetual maintenance of an inclined runway eight feet, five inches wide connecting the stable yard, which is on the cellar level, with Mount Vernon Street, through which the occupants of the 'adjacent tenements [referring to the three Chestnut Street houses] are to have the right of ingress and egress for themselves and their cattle.' The popular misunderstanding of these latter terms has been that a right of way was here granted for a cow. Possibly cows may have been kept by the original families, but the word 'cattle' in this connection doubtless included horses, the stabling for which was in the basement with carriage rooms on the Mount Vernon Street level.

It will be recalled that while these things were going on in upper Chestnut Street, Mr. Otis, Mr. Mason, Mr. Callender, and Mr. Perkins built their residences on Mount Vernon Street, and that Mr. Mason and Stephen Higginson, Jr., each built a block of houses on the north side of the same street just west of Joy. The north side of upper Pinckney Street was also building up at this time. All else on the Hill, from the ridge crest to the river, and south to Beacon Street, was still wild pasture, except where the Proprietors were engaged in grading down the bluffs from the site of Louisburg Square to Charles Street. By 1805 the latter street had been graded up along the old shore front and six houses were built between Beacon and Branch Streets. In those days the latter was known as Kitchen Street because it served the rear entrances of the houses on Beacon and Chestnut Streets. One year earlier the brick Phillips house had been built on the lower corner of Beacon and Walnut Streets, next above the old Copley houses, and at the same time four residences were erected on the Beacon Street lots next above Spruce Street by a group of builders, William Homer, G. W. Otis, Jonathan Thaxter, and George Sprague. These were assessed as 'four new houses' in 1805.

On the lower corner of Spruce Street, Samuel Alleyne Otis, father of Harrison Gray Otis, for thirty years Secretary of the United States Senate, built a house for himself which was assessed as 'unfinished' in 1805. He lived there until his death in 1813. Those five houses covered the sites of Numbers 46 to 50, and apparently the only vestige remaining of these buildings is a part of the brick walls of Number 49. Between 1806 and 1809 eight other houses were built below Spruce Street. Jeremiah Gardner and Peter Osgood, housewrights, who built a number of houses large and small on various parts of the Hill, broke ground for Number 51 in 1805. The next year Thomas Kendall, a fashionable tailor, built 52 and 53; James Colburn, a Kilby Street merchant, 54 and 55; Asher Benjamin, housewright and architect, 58; and John Cotton, house painter, 60. Daniel Tuttle, brickmason, built 59 in 1809, and this was the last house erected in that block until nearly a dozen years later. Meantime Harrison Gray Otis had finished his mansion in 1806 in the block above, at Number 45. This house, doubtless planned by Bulfinch, was assessed that year as an 'elegant new house,' but it is stated that the builder designated it in language something less than elegant, though, from his point of view, fully descriptive. The writer has the story direct from one of the older residents of the Hill that, on the completion of the mansion, a sheaf of itemized accounts was rendered to Mr. Otis, who protested that he had no time to examine these in detail and asked that a

171

bill for the full amount be submitted. Borrowing pen and paper, the builder thereupon figured up the total and wrote out a bill reading: 'To Harrison Gray Otis, for one damn great house,' so many dollars. Unfortunately the price did not make a sufficiently strong impression to have been remembered, but the assessors valued it that same year at twenty thousand dollars. The accuracy of this story has been questioned by Samuel Eliot Morison, Otis's biographer, on the ground that Mr. Otis was most punctilious in all money matters and exceedingly particular as to outgo. Possibly the bill was thus facetiously rendered, but there is nothing in the story to prove that Mr. Otis did not again object, this time on the ground that it was too generalized and unbusinesslike.

Only two of those early houses below Spruce Street remain. These are Colburn's houses, 54 and 55, the latter the residence of William Hickling Prescott, the historian, from 1845 to 1859. They are but little altered in outward appearance and are strikingly handsome houses with graceful balanced bow fronts spanned by a balcony, supported by a colonnade, with Corinthian pilasters rising to the cornice. Who the architect was does not seem to be known, though the guess has been hazarded that it was Asher Benjamin. Mr. Colburn lived in Number 55 for many years, but 54 he sold to Nathan Appleton in 1808 for $13,500.

After business conditions had begun to recover from the effects of the War of 1812, Ephraim Marsh, one of the well-known builder-architects of his day, bought the site of 62 Beacon Street in 1819, and built a house which he sold to the wife of Henry G. Rice. That autumn, Marsh bought the lots now numbered 56 and 57. The latter he sold the following spring to David Eckley for $3250 and at the same time contracted to build a house for him there for $13,000. Marsh furnished the plans and found all the materials except the parlor and drawing-room chimney pieces. The recorded contract states that Marsh was at the time at work on Number 62 for Mr. Rice, and certain features of the Eckley house were specified to be like those in the Rice residence. The specifications covering two features of the Eckley house are suggestive of the comparative primitiveness of the time. Here was a high-class residence in a fashionable quarter, and it and its next-door counterpart, Number 56, rank among the handsome houses along the Common front to-day. The contract provided for stone cornices and handsome interior finish, also that 'In the cellar there is to be a bathing room in front into which the aqueduct is to be led,' and that the pump in the back yard is to have a box 'to hang meat in.'

The only other record found of early plumbing is that connected with the installation of flush closets in the basement of the State House in 1825. When this innovation was proposed to a committee of the Governor's Council, that body assumed a most conservative attitude, and finally returned a report in which they expressed their unanimous opinion as follows: 'Although such closets may be much approved of in private dwelling houses, it admits of doubt at least whether all these advantages can be expected and realized in so public a place as the State House, where visits to them must of necessity be frequent and by persons unaccustomed to their use.'

Until that time the sanitary conveniences connected with the State House had been confined to vaults in the yard at the westerly end of the main building. Messrs. Coolidge and Hubbard, who were developing the Hancock land adjoining, and building houses there for sale, desired that the vaults should be removed and volunteered to install the closets at their own expense in return for the favor sought. In spite of the foregoing adverse report, the petition was finally admitted, but only after Mr. Coolidge had agreed to furnish a bond in the penal sum of five thousand dollars, obliging him to remove the closets and to restore the vaults at his own cost, if, within three years, the Legislature found the former to be what the Council termed 'inadequate.' The Legislature evidently never objected to the arrangement, but the minutes of the entire discussion were for some reason made a matter of public record, and may be found in Suffolk Deeds (L. 307, f. 273).

Marsh sold Number 56 to William Howard Eliot, who sold it in 1831 to the children of John Lowell, Jr., the founder of the Lowell Institute lectures. It is said that on the occasion of one of Lafayette's visits to Boston a ball was given in his honor at this house. William Minot built 61, Tasker H. Swett 63, and, finally, in 1824, John Bryant built 64 at the end of the block. Early in July of the latter year, just as Bryant's house was finishing, a fire broke out in the carpenter shops located in the rear, and before it could be controlled the six houses on Charles Street, the first seven on Beacon Street above the alley, and Numbers 62 and 64 Chestnut Street were consumed. The memory of this spectacular fire was still vivid with Mr. Bowditch when he wrote his final 'Gleaner' article in January, 1856. The fire broke out about two in the afternoon on July 7th and Mr. Bowditch, then a young man, hearing the alarm, was early on the scene. It must have been a terrifying spectacle, for by the time that he arrived a mass of flame, driven by a high northwest wind, was belching from the alley and sweeping completely across Beacon Street to the Common, where it shriveled the trees along the mall. The fire was finally checked at Mr. Eckley's house, Number 57. The assessors' records show that the taxes were abated on all of the burned houses that year. That they were immediately rebuilt is witnessed by the tax list for 1825 which describes all the houses as 'unfinished.' An interesting reminder of that fire was uncovered a few years ago incidental to the work of repairing the front door of the house built by Mr. Bryant, Number 64 Beacon Street. One of the carved cornerblocks of the architrave inside the door was removed, and on its back the carpenter discovered the following notation in pencil: 'Repaired by [illegible name, apparently Italian] this 25th day of July 1825 on account of a fire. We had some rum punch today.'

While these developments were progressing, and just before the fire, changes were being made in the block above. In 1816, Daniel P. Parker, a prominent shipping merchant, and Nathan Appleton, who was associated with Francis C. Lowell and Patrick T. Jackson in the development of cotton manufactures, bought the upper Copley house on the sites of 39 and 40 Beacon Street, then occupied by the Cushing family (L. 252, f. 70; L. 263, f. 90). This they removed, and in 1819 completed the handsome houses that still stand on that lot, Number 40 being the house of the Women's City Club. These houses are supposed to have been designed by Bulfinch. Just before they were finished, Colonel David Sears purchased the lot next west, with the old house in which it is believed Copley lived, and until then long occupied by John Vinal. Colonel Sears paid twenty thousand dollars for this property (L. 259, f. 193), demolished the old house and began the erection of a fine stone mansion, a portion of which remains in the easterly bow of the Somerset Club, 42 Beacon Street. The tax records show that Colonel Sears was assessed in 1819 for a vacant lot, indicating that he had then removed the Vinal house. In both 1820 and 1821 the assessors entered the property as an 'unfinished house,' but in 1822 the owner was taxed as living there. The original house, designed by Alexander Parris, a Boston architect and engineer, who modeled it to some extent, so it is said, after the mansion of Colonel Sears's father-in-law, Jonathan Mason, on Mount Vernon Street, is shown in the drawing here reproduced. On the east, toward Mr. Parker's house, a driveway entered to the entrance portico and to the stable in the rear. On the west was a garden adjoining the garden of Mr. Otis. The easterly bow of the Otis house, looking out upon the garden, is shown in the drawing of the Sears mansion.

In 1831, Colonel Sears bought of Mr. Otis a strip of that garden twenty-five feet wide on the street, and the following spring the assessors found both gentlemen 'erecting' houses that covered the entire area between the two former houses. This was the origin of 44 Beacon Street, built by Mr. Otis, and of the westerly end of the Somerset Club with its second bow, now Number 43, built by Colonel Sears. Both of these new houses were assessed as 'empty' in 1833, and 44 was called 'vacant' in 1834. In that year Colonel Sears's son-in-law, William Amory, was assessed as living at 43, and a year later Francis C. Gray was a tenant in 44. After two years Mr. Gray was succeeded by Samuel Austin, who continued there until after Mr. Otis's death when he bought 45, where he was assessed as living in 1854. Robert Gould Shaw, Jr., bought 44 of the Otis heirs at the same time. Mr. Amory lived at 43 from 1834 until 1852, in which year the assessors found him at 41. This latter house had been built by Colonel Sears, in 1838 and 1839, for another son-in-law, George C. Crowninshield, who lived there until 1852. On Mr. Amory's moving to 41, a third son-in-law, William C. Rives, Jr., took 43. After the death of Colonel Sears, these properties were bought by the Somerset Club in 1871. Extensive alterations, mainly within and in the rear, were made at that time from plans by Snell and Gregerson, and it is the opinion of architects that the third story was then added to the stone house. A tablet set in an interior wall of the original mansion, Number 42, at the time of its building, bears an inscription to the effect that it was built from designs by Alex-

ander Parris in 1819. This was doubtless the year
in which it was begun. Record evidence already
referred to shows that it was not completed before
the summer of 1821. It is stated on good authority
that the decorative panels on the Beacon Street
wall of this house, and presumably those on the
addition of 1832, Number 43, were carved by
Solomon Willard. He was best known as the
architect of the Bunker Hill Monument. He was
also associated with Parris in the construction,
in 1819, of Saint Paul's Church, now the Episcopal
Cathedral, on Tremont Street. While the alterations of 1871 in the Sears mansion were in progress
a secret compartment was uncovered in the attic of
the old house, and in it was found a forgotten stock
of old Madeira wine.

Between 1806 and 1812 fifteen other houses were
built on the Copley pasture. These were located on
Walnut, Chestnut, and Mount Vernon Streets.
Number 2 Chestnut and 11 and 13 Walnut appear
to have been built in 1806. Two years later, John
Howe built 42 Chestnut, four doors below Spruce
Street, and its next-door neighbor, 44, was one of
Jeremiah Gardner's houses, built in 1810. Farther
down on the same side of that street, opposite West
Cedar, 62 was built in 1811 by Joseph Lincoln and
Hezekiah Stoddard, housewrights. They also
built 64, but not until 1817. As already stated,
those houses were burned in 1824 and their rebuild-

ing was not completed until 1826. Mr. Lincoln himself lived at Number 62 at that time, and Mr. Stoddard at 64. In 1827, they built Number 66 and sold it to Thomas W. Phillips. The following year they built 68, which remained in the ownership of the Stoddard family until 1842.

Gardner was busy on Mount Vernon Street and on upper Chestnut Street between 1808 and 1810. In the former year he bought of Benjamin Joy the Mount Vernon Street end of the lot between the Theological School and Willow Street. This he cut into house lots, which were almost immediately sold for prices ranging from twelve hundred to two thousand dollars. Moses Grant, Sr., the upholstery dealer, built a house for his own occupancy at 74 Mount Vernon Street next to the school, then Derby's stable, in 1810. Cornelius Coolidge, the architect, was a son-in-law of Mr. Grant. Numbers 76 and 78 were built on speculation by carpenters the following year, as was 86 in 1812. Numbers 80, 82, and 84 do not appear to have had houses until about 1822. In 1809, when Gardner sold the sites of 76, 78, and 80, he reserved the right 'to remove the buildings off said land that are now on the same.' No one can tell to-day what the nature of these buildings may have been, but one might be permitted to indulge in a guess that they were small frame structures, perhaps used by Gardner as carpenter shops. Gardner's deeds stipulated in some instances that only three-story brick dwellings should be built on these lots; in other cases that no ten-foot buildings, except necessary outbuildings, should be erected. On the site of Number 84 the restriction was that 'no building shall ever˙be erected thereon except of brick or stone and more than ten feet high.'

As soon as Gardner had disposed of those lots, he bought the land next east of Derby from Mr. Otis and at once began building houses on the sites of 23 and 25 Chestnut Street. The sites of 66 and 68 Mount Vernon Street he sold to John Osborn. His deed in this case is dated September 13, 1808, and, judging from the price named, ten thousand dollars, buildings must have been included. Notwithstanding this, the assessors named Gardner as the owner in 1809 and noted the property as being a vacant lot. In 1810, however, two rented houses were taxed there to Osborn at five thousand dollars each, the tenant being Daniel Weeks, grocer, in 66, and Jesse Sumner, merchant, in 68. From this and several other similar cases it is inferred that Osborn, who was a prosperous paint importer, frequently financed Gardner's building enterprises, and in some instances took over the property on completion. Number 66 remained in the Osborn family through three generations. John Trecothick Apthorp, president of the Boston Bank, owned the two lots below the Swan stables, 62 and 64, and built on one of these a house in which he was assessed as living in 1809, and the other, apparently, in the following year.

The remainder of that entire section of the Hill was, for the most part, built up between 1821 and 1830, though a few lots on Mount Vernon Street near West Cedar, and on the latter street as well, were not built upon until the Louisburg Square development began in the thirties. John Hubbard and Cornelius Coolidge were particularly active at this time. No evidence has been found to show that a formal partnership existed between these men, but, wherever Hubbard was engaged in a development, Coolidge's name is usually closely associated with it. One instance has been found where they were jointly taxed for a house of their construction. It has been previously noted that both men were prominently connected with the building operations on the Hancock estate in the twenties.

The supposition is that Hubbard was the capitalist in these instances and that Coolidge was the architect. It is clear, however, that Coolidge not infrequently undertook developments on his own account. At first he seems to have let out his building enterprises by contract to mechanics, and a number of these documents are on record with Suffolk Deeds. In the thirties he entered the contracting field himself, as in the building of the houses on the site of Dr. John Joy's homestead lot on Beacon and Joy Streets.

Harrison Gray Otis took a hand in stimulating the building of the early twenties by putting up houses on some of the lots that fell to his portion in the syndicate distributions. Thus, in 1822, he built 22 and 24 Chestnut Street, two houses with dignified classical porticoes. These he sold the next year to Edward Blanchard for $20,500, and Mr. Blanchard in turn deeded them to his daughters, who had married brothers, Joshua and Lot Wheelwright, Jr. When Louisburg Square was laid out in 1826, Mr. Otis built two houses on the lower corner of Willow and Mount Vernon Streets, facing the Square. The other lots in that block, like those on the Square, were slow to move, however. Finally, in 1832, Theodore M. Bowker built 104 Mount Vernon Street, on the corner of West Cedar, the house that in recent years was the residence of the late Professor Percival Lowell, the authority on Martian astronomy. The remainder of the block was built up between 1833 and 1837 by various persons.

Madam Swan's town residence in Chestnut Street, opposite her three daughters, has already been referred to. This house, Number 16, is of a type that suggests an earlier date than is borne out by the records. In 1821 the sites of 12, 14, and 16 were assessed to Mrs. Swan's trustee as three lots, the next year as two lots and an unfinished house, and the next as two occupied houses and one house unfinished. In 1823 and 1824, Number 16 was assessed as the residence of 'Hepzibah Swan, Lady,' with the notation that she went out of town May 1st, which presumably indicated that she spent her summers at her Dorchester mansion. By a careful tracing of the titles to those three houses it is found that 12 and 16 were finished first, that the former was sold to Ebenezer Sage, and that the latter was taken by Mrs. Swan, while Benjamin Welles rented 14 when completed, but later, after Mrs. Swan's death, bought 16 and moved there.

It has already been stated that Cornelius Coolidge built Numbers 4 and 10 Chestnut Street in 1825. The rest of that block to Spruce Street was built up by various persons, Jesse Shaw, one of the best builders of the period (who began as a journeyman under Jeremiah Gardner), William Lancaster, and Isaac Davenport being responsible for several, and mostly in 1821 and 1822. On the opposite side of the street, between the three early Swan houses and Walnut Street, there were large lots running through to Mount Vernon Street. One of these pieces, next to the Swan houses, was taken by John Hubbard, who built six houses there in 1824, three on each street, from plans by Coolidge. These are among the best examples of

Coolidge's handiwork. Ephraim Marsh took up the lots cornering on Walnut Street in 1821. On the Mount Vernon Street frontage he built, in 1822, a mansion house for John Heard, Jr., which was sold to Augustus Hemenway in 1849. Mr. Hemenway demolished the old house, and in 1850 built the brownstone houses now numbered 40 and 42, the World Peace Foundation, from plans by George M. Dexter. Marsh also built that same year Numbers 1, 3, and 5 Chestnut Street, and the upper two have survived substantially as built.

Mr. Hubbard took a prominent part in the up-building of the south side of Chestnut Street below Spruce, the six houses from 50 to 60 having been built by him in 1824. No evidence has been found to prove that they were planned by Coolidge, but their architectural details suggest that he did. Coolidge himself built 70 to 76, near Charles Street, in 1828. The first house above Charles Street, on the opposite side of Chestnut, Number 61, was built in 1825 by Bela Stoddard, a relative of Hezekiah. This was in 1827, and these were the last built in that block. At the same time Hubbard was building the entire block on the westerly side of West Cedar Street, between Mount Vernon and Chestnut Streets. In 1827 and also in 1828 and 1829, Coolidge built 39 to 45 and 55 Chestnut Street, on the north side, next below Willow Street, and 1 to 5 Acorn Street. Lee and Leighton, builders, were accountable for 49 Chestnut Street in 1827, and for 47 in 1830, while the next two houses west, 51 and 53, were by Benjamin and Hiram Bosworth. The corner house at West Cedar Street was built for Samuel Snelling in 1828. The lower three houses on Acorn Street and the adjoining house facing West Cedar date from 1828 and 1829. The other three houses on that side of West Cedar Street, north of Acorn Street, were not built until 1833 and 1834. Asher Benjamin, the architect, built Number 9 for his own occupancy.

With few exceptions the houses in the section covered by this chapter stand to-day substantially as when they were built so far as outward appearances are concerned. In some instances the original entrance doors were changed to the glass-paneled double-door type popular half a century ago. In quite recent years a few of these have been replaced with reproductions of the best examples of the older period.

XIII

LOUISBURG SQUARE

IN the spring of 1796, after the Mount Vernon Proprietors had finally settled the differences with the Copley family as to the price of that land, and were in full possession of this and of the Allen lot on the north side of Mount Vernon Street, they proceeded at once with plans for development. Osgood Carleton, the foremost surveyor in Boston in his day, had previously made a plan of the Copley land, very likely as a basis for the deed to that property. The new owners now called in another surveyor, Mather Withington, of Dorchester, to produce a street plan. That lay-out provided for Mount Vernon, Chestnut, and Walnut Streets as they now are, and suggested Pinckney Street. It also cut up the intervening land into house lots, but only as far west as Spruce Street and Louisburg Square, neither of which was so much as hinted at on that drawing.

Thirty years later, the Proprietors decided to open the lands west of the David Humphreys house, 89 Mount Vernon Street. Apparently Mr. Bulfinch's earlier conception of a garden square had been lurking in the minds of the Proprietors

all these years, and possibly they inspired S. P.
Fuller, their surveyor at this time, with the idea
of Louisburg Square. Fuller's plan was drawn in
April, 1826, and on the first of June of that year
the Proprietors entered into an agreement by
which all of the area bounded by the house lots on
the easterly side of Louisburg Square, by West
Cedar Street, by the northerly side of Mount
Vernon Street below the Square, and by the lots
on the north side of Pinckney Street west from the
school to West Cedar, was laid out in streets and
lots, the latter being divided in severalty among
the members of the syndicate. That indenture
did not go to record until September 7th, however,
and none of this land was moved in the market
until eight years thereafter. The pending suits of
the Overseers of the Poor, which involved a chal-
lenge of the title to the lots just west of the Square,
and to some of those on the north side of Pinckney
Street, may have tended to discourage purchases.
It was under the terms of that Proprietors' agreement that the 'Square or open space . . . and the
streets parallel therewith' were 'forever reserved
for that purpose, provided that the part designated for the square may be surrounded with an
open fence or railing.' It was also provided that
the streets should be 'ceded to the city government
as such whenever they will accept the same.'
This provision did not meet with the approval of

the purchasers of those house lots, however, as will shortly be seen, at least in so far as Louisburg Square was concerned, and that has remained a private way to the present day and under the control of the abutting property-owners.

It has already been seen that in the early eighteen-thirties a building boom began on the Hill. Many of the houses on the north side of Mount Vernon Street, between the Square and Walnut Street, were built at that time, and Israel Thorndike and Cornelius Coolidge were also busy on the site of Dr. Joy's homestead at the corner of Beacon and Joy Streets. This renewed interest in building brought the Square into the market, and on August 20, 1834, the first lot was sold there to John Clark, who at once built a house on the upper Pinckney Street corner, now 19 Louisburg Square. That lot, thirty-five feet wide by about seventy-five feet deep, sold for $2092. Later this was the home for seventeen years of Mayor Frederick W. Lincoln. During the next three or four years most of the other lots on the upper and lower sides of the Square were sold, several of them to building contractors who erected houses on speculation.

Jesse Shaw was one of the most active of these builders, his first venture being the purchase of the lot now 22 Louisburg Square, on the lower corner of Pinckney. For this lot, about twenty-two by eighty feet, he paid the Mason family $2936 in February, 1835, and in July of that year he sold the house which he built there to Miss Lydia White, of Haverhill, for $14,500. In April, 1835, the Swan Estate sold a lot, now Number 8, to Phineas Upham, who built a house and sold it in October to Andrew C. Fearing for $14,500. The following spring Mr. Fearing and his wife, whose name was Aldeberontophoscophonia, sold for $15,250 to the Reverend John Codman, of Dorchester.. Among the other early houses were Numbers 7, 9, and 17 on the upper side, and 8, 10, and 12 on the lower side. These, according to the best belief of the Proprietors' Committee, were built in 1835. Numbers 14 to 20 on the west side were probably built in 1836, and 11 to 17 on the east side between 1836 and 1839. Number 7 was built by Sampson Reed, one of the early expounders of the doctrines of Swedenborg and father of the Reverend James Reed, for many years pastor of the Church of the New Jerusalem. His daughter Elizabeth, who was born in that house, continued to live there until her death in 1918. The next house, Number 9, was built by the Reverend Thomas Worcester, the first Swedenborgian minister in Boston. George W. Pratt, who took Number 13 in 1839, lived there for the remainder of his life, and was succeeded by his son Robert, who died there in 1917. For some reason the six lots at the southerly ends of the Square did not sell as readily as the others. Numbers 4, 5, and 6 were built about 1842, but 1, 2, and 3 were not taken up until nearly five years later. Thomas Handasyd Perkins, Jr., who lived at 1 Joy Street, built 2 Louisburg Square in 1847 and sold it to James P. Higginson, whose daughter was the wife of William I. Bowditch, son of 'Gleaner.'

Early in the summer of 1844, the Square having been fully built up except for the two lots on the Mount Vernon Street corners and the one next to the corner on the upper side, the house-owners held a meeting at Mr. Clark's, Number 19, to consider a proposal for a 'widening of the mall in the Square and surrounding the same with a new fence or railing.' According to the original indenture of 1826, the syndicate agreed to lay out 'the oval in the Square' at their expense. Presumably they surrounded the plot with a fence at that time, very likely a simple affair of neat wooden posts and squared rails. Not improbably they grassed the enclosure also, but whether they set out the elms around the border is not known. There is nothing in the records of the Proprietors' Committee, which was an outgrowth of this meeting, to indicate the date of the tree-planting, but there is a possibility that the trees were set out as a part of the programme proposed at that gathering which was to 'enlarge and adorn said Square for the mutual advantage and enjoyment of said parties being such owners.' The immediate result of the meeting was the appointment of a committee consisting of Samuel A. Dorr, James H. Adams, and John Clark.

Less than one month later, July 8, 1844, an agreement was entered into between the committee and the following-named neighbors: Harrison Gray Otis and John C. Warren (presumably representing the Mount Vernon Proprietors, owners of the remaining vacant lots), Thomas W. Ward, William Parsons, John Bryant, Jr., Ammi C. Lombard, John Codman, Jesse Shaw, Francis Welch, Samuel Neal, Eliza Goodwin, Sampson Reed, Thomas Worcester, Abiel Washburn, George W. Pratt, Benjamin Burgess, Philip R. Southwick, George R. Minot, Franklin Burgess, Nathan B. Gibbs, James S. Savage, and Thomas Lord. It was there recited that these owners propose to enlarge and adorn the Square, and that they agree mutually to bear the cost of the work, provided that the expense shall not exceed one hundred and fifty dollars per lot. Furthermore, it was agreed that the cost of future repairs and embellishments to 'the ground enclosed within the Square' should be similarly assessable upon the abutting properties, which includes the houses on Pinckney Street facing the Square, but not those similarly placed on Mount Vernon Street. Moreover, they bound themselves to include these terms in any subsequent conveyances of the several properties. Finally, for the orderly transaction of the joint business interests of the parties, it was provided that meetings of the owners might be called at any time upon the written notice of any three, and that the votes and doings of a majority of those present should be binding upon all parties. The appointment of a clerk, 'as often as seems fit,' was called for, that suitable records of the meetings might be kept. Under these simple by-laws the Proprietors' organization has continued successfully for eighty years.

Just when these proposed improvements were carried out cannot be stated, but on the last day of December, 1846, the committee in charge reported to a meeting of the Proprietors that the grassed area had been lengthened ten feet and widened eight feet, also that an iron fence had been erected. It was at this meeting that the houses on the Square were assigned their numbers, and the first standing committee authorized, Francis Welch, Jesse Shaw, Nathan B. Gibbs, Jr., and B. F. Burgess being chosen. Since that time many men whose names are familiar to residents on the Hill have served on that committee. The longest terms are credited to George W. Pratt, who was a member for twenty years previous to his death in 1876; to his son Robert M. Pratt, who served from 1881 until his death in 1917; and to Benjamin B. Williams, whose term of twenty-three years was terminated by his death in 1906. Those who have served as clerk, with their dates, are as follows: John Clark, 1844–52; George W. Pratt, 1856 and 1860–70; Samuel F. McCleary (the first city clerk), 1857–59; William P. Kuhn, 1871–89; during which time John T. Heard acted pro tempore 1882–88; Benjamin B. Williams, 1890–1906; Hobart W. Winkley, 1906–24. The treasurers' list is somewhat longer: B. F. Burgess, 1845–52; S. F. McCleary, 1856–59; Nathaniel Walker, 1860; William Hilton, 1861–69; Thomas Minns, 1870; William S. Eaton, 1871–76; Hamilton Willis, 1877; W. P. Kuhn, 1878; William T. Parker, 1879–88; J. Theodore Heard, 1889–98; Alexander Wadsworth, 1899–1906; Henry R. Heard, 1906–17 and 1920–24; Dwight Prouty, 1918; J. Colby Bassett, 1919.

Shortly after the fencing of the Square had been carried out, Joseph Iasigi became a resident at Number 3. Very likely the trim enclosure in front of his house seemed Puritanically cold and bare to him in its unrelieved greensward and trees. At all events, it was not long thereafter that he notified the Proprietors that he had lately received from Florence a marble statue of Aristides the Just, which it would be his pleasure to erect within the mall if acceptable to his neighbors, and invited an inspection of the work at his place of business.

LOUISBURG SQUARE

Nearly a year later, in October, 1850, the gift of the statue was formally accepted and a special committee, consisting of Mr. Iasigi, Thomas Lord, and John Clark, was appointed to arrange not only for the setting of this new ornament, but to provide in addition a similar statue of Columbus and a fountain. It is related that the two statues came out from Italy as part of the ballast of a ship consigned to Boston.

The records of the Square Proprietors do not reveal when these improvements were completed. There is the mention of the fact that the fountain was ordered in October, 1850. Then in January, 1852, it is written that a committee was directed to confer with the city authorities as to a supply of water for the fountain. And, finally, on April 16, 1856, there is the vote directing that the reservoir in the center of the Square be filled up and planted with flowers. Fortunately some one has preserved a letter through all these years that tells the story in brief. On November 9, 1850, Miss Eliza Goodwin, one of the original Proprietors, who lived at Number 5, wrote to her brother in Maine that 'the fountain is now playing for the second time, last Saturday the first, and it looks quite well, but I cannot tell what it will cost as yet. It has taken six weeks to prepare the basin.'

Either because the youthful population of that period had shown a disposition to use the enclosure

as a playground, or because there was some sus-
picion that these unwonted street adornments
might inspire boyish prankishness, the Proprietors
voted, in 1852, that boys should not be tolerated
within the fence, and forbidding them 'to injure
or meddle with any of the embellishments of the
same.' To insure the enforcement of these regula-
tions the Proprietors as a whole were given such
measure of police power as the meeting could lawfully bestow. In spite of this mandate and the
iron fence, a small boy once managed to elude the
watchfulness of the neighborhood, and, either in
defiance or by accident, deprived Columbus of an
index finger. And then the enormity of his crime
loomed up before him and, terror-stricken, he
dashed down the hill and cast the evidence of his
guilt into the waters of the Charles.

Although the fountain long since disappeared,
the statues still grace the ends of the mall, having
escaped any further mutilation at the hands of
small boys or even by the elements. For some years
in recent times it was the custom of the Italian
societies to visit the Square on Columbus Day for
the purpose of decorating the effigy of their distinguished national with wreaths. Since 1920 this
ceremony has been abandoned. There was a brief
period also, during which a Technology fraternity
occupied Number 6 on the westerly side of the
Square, when Aristides was occasionally the recipi-

ent of decorative attentions at the hands of the students. Now that the Tech boys no longer frequent the Square, the noble Greek wears no laurels on festal occasions.

The fountain was set up two years after Cochituate water was introduced into the city. Possibly the Proprietors found it difficult to secure an adequate supply for this ornamental use at a reasonable price. Possibly the city authorities felt that it was politically inexpedient to furnish water for the mere adornment of a neighborhood so exclusive that the right of public passage through its streets was denied except as a matter of sufferance. Perhaps a search of the records of the Water Department would disclose the real cause of the discontinuance. Could they have revived that ancient spring, which once flowed copiously at the northerly end of the present grassed area, and believed by some antiquaries to have been Blaxton's historic supply, and that later was the dependence of the colored wash-women of the Hill, there might have been water enough and to spare.

After much searching and the making of many inquiries, a picture of the Square as it was in the early fifties has been found, and thanks to its fortunate possessor, who is a resident of the Square, its reproduction is permitted here. This drawing appeared in the issue of 'Gleason's Pictorial

Drawing Room Companion,' published in Boston, May 31, 1857, which was a year and one month after the fountain had been ordered abolished according to the record quoted above. Possibly the order was not carried out with dispatch. Most things were done with greater deliberation in those days. Possibly the publisher of 'Gleason's,' having spent good money for the picture, felt disinclined to junk the cut even if it was a trifle out of date. Or perhaps the editor's pride of authorship in the explanatory paragraphs which appeared above the picture dulled his news sensibilities. Be that as it may, both the picture and its accompanying text are interesting to-day not merely because they describe an interesting feature of the Hill now long past, but also as a specimen of the high-class journalism of that period. To print the picture without the legend would be altogether wasteful of the local color. This is what the editor of 'Gleason's' wrote about the Square:

The engraving below represents a beautiful location in the western section of our city, surrounded by the residences of many of our most distinguished and fashionable families. This place affords one among many evidences that taste and refinement are gradually beautifying our city, and by and by Boston will present many out-door specimens of the fine arts worthy of her character as the literary emporium and Athens of America.

A very fine statue of Columbus, about six feet high,

LOUISBURG SQUARE AS IT WAS IN THE FIFTIES

From a woodcut in *Gleason's Drawing Room Companion*

and of Italian workmanship, has recently been set up in the Square. It is placed at the northern extremity of the enclosure, while the southern end is ornamented by a statue of Aristides the Just, and the centre by a beautiful fountain. The whole is surrounded by trees, and enclosed with a handsome fence, and involved an expense of not much less than $6000, which has been borne by the adjoining proprietors.

We heartily rejoice at the spirit that induces these liberal outlays for such purposes as we have named, believing that such displays are not without a refining and beneficial influence upon the masses, and are well calculated to cultivate intelligence and good taste.

It was at this time that the Proprietors seem to have definitely decided that they did not care to carry out the original intent of the former land syndicate which contemplated conveying the streets of the Square to the city. At the January meeting, in 1852, a committee was named to consider the expediency of perpetuating the legal rights of the abuttors by barricading the Square against public passage for a sufficient period to prevent the establishment of any public easement through uncontested user. That they decided this question in the affirmative is shown by the record that, on November 2, 1855, notice was served upon the Board of Aldermen that the Square was closed to public travel 'to preserve the right of the Proprietors in and to said property, and to prevent said Square and streets being dedicated as public property.' That in itself might have supplied

sufficient provocation for a denial of any extra-
ordinary water privileges for the benefit of a mere
fountain. If that was the attitude of City Hall, it
had no influence upon the people of the Square in
their desire to manage their streets for themselves,
and twenty years later, in November, 1875, bar-
riers were again raised and notice given that these
were private ways. At the end of the next twenty-
year period, in August, 1895, a new method was
resorted to. Instead of barricading the streets,
notices were posted on the corners and in the
center of the Square by a deputy sheriff, where
they were maintained for six successive days, after
which a copy of the notice was recorded with
Suffolk Deeds and the action was thus made
permanent. Only once did the city attempt an
encroachment in violation of the private claim.
Probably through some inadvertence a voting
booth was set up within the limits of the Square,
but after the election the Proprietors presented
a bill for ground rent to the city and the incident
was thereby closed.

Although the Square can boast no Bulfinch
houses, and is much more modern than some other
sections of the Hill, its retired charm and English
flavor make it one of the most attractive features
of the section. During its something less than
ninety years of existence, many men and women
of note have lived there. One of the earliest social

events of wide importance enacted there was the marriage of the famous singer, Jenny Lind, to her accompanist, Otto Goldschmidt, on February 5, 1852. Samuel G. Ward, who lived at Number 20, was Boston representative of Baring Brothers, the prima-donna's London bankers, and he opened his house for the occasion. During her most successful years Louisa M. Alcott and her aged father lived as tenants at Number 10, and William Dean Howells was at Number 4 at the time when he was editing the 'Atlantic Monthly.' In the sixties John G. Palfrey, author of 'The History of New England,' was a tenant in the Square, and the well-beloved Reverend Samuel Hobart Winkley made his home at Number 11 from 1874 until his death in 1911. In the summer of 1915, Mrs. Fiske, the celebrated actress, chose the Square as the setting for a scene from 'Vanity Fair' that she was to act before a screen camera. It was to be the picture of the marriage of Becky Sharp to Jos Sedley in Russell Square, London, and in Louisburg Mrs. Fiske found an environment sufficiently English in its qualities to satisfy the needs of the occasion. In this act she was supported by two amateurs, both residents of the Square, one gentleman taking the part of Sedley, the other, arrayed in blue-and-white livery, acted as coachman and drove the bride and groom around the mall.

Much searching of records, and many inquiries made through persons long associated with the Hill, have failed positively to reveal the reason for giving the name Louisburg to the Square. In the indenture of the Mount Vernon Proprietors laying out this section in 1826, which is recorded with Suffolk Deeds, the name does not appear, the enclosure being referred to as 'the square.' On Fuller's original plan of the lay-out, also in the Registry, the name is lettered across the oval of the little park, indicating plainly that it was given at the beginning.

It is natural to presume that the name commemorates one or both of the Provincial campaigns against the Cape Breton stronghold of Louisburg, and following that clue an attempt has been made to trace a definite reason. No dates connected with the early history of the Square fell on an anniversary of either of the sieges, and no one connected with the families of the Mount Vernon Proprietors has been discovered who was a participant in either of those engagements. Louisburg was first captured by Sir William Pepperell June 17, 1745. It fell the second time July 27, 1758, to the forces under Lord Amherst. It is suggested by Mr. Julian Tuttle, of the Massachusetts Historical Society, that possibly the dedication of the monument at Bunker Hill in 1825 caused some one to note that the battles of Louisburg had never been recognized by any memorial, and that the Proprietors were moved to perpetuate the name in this way. Dr. Samuel Eliot Morison entertains no doubt but that the name commemorates the campaign of 1745, which was planned and carried out by the New-Englanders, Boston taking a leading part in the enterprise. In answer to the writer's inquiries on this subject, Dr. Morison replied: 'Paris has its Place des Victoires, its Rue des Pyrénées, and London its Waterloo Bridge. Why not Boston its Louisburg Square?'

The nearest approach to a definite reason for associating the name of Louisburg with the Square is found in a biographical sketch of William Blaxton by Thomas Coffin Amory, which was printed as a pamphlet in 1877. It is there stated that 'The son of our William had sons, one of whom, a lieutenant, fell at the siege of Louisburg in 1746.' The date is doubtless a misprint. Unfortunately Mr. Amory cited no authority for this statement, nor did he make any allusion whatever to this soldier grandson of the first settler in a paper on Blaxton that he read before the Bostonian Society in 1880.[1] Lucius Manlius Sargent's paper on the Blaxton family, first printed in the 'Boston Transcript' in 1849,[2] and James Savage's

[1] Bostonian Society Publications, vol. I, p. 19.
[2] Reprinted, Norwich, Connecticut, 1857.

'Genealogical Dictionary' of 1860, are both silent upon this point. The military records of the 1745 campaign [1] have been carefully searched, but no Blaxton or Blackstone is found there.

It is not impossible that this tradition or fact, whichever it may be, was known to the Proprietors in 1826. If such was the case, the naming of the Square was singularly appropriate, since it is unquestionably located on a part of the Blaxton six-acre lot, and some believe that his famous spring flowed not far from where the Columbus statue stands.

At one time there seems to have existed some difference of opinion as to the correct spelling of the name. The fact that Fuller, the surveyor, spelled it 'Louisburg' in lettering it upon his plan would seem to have set a standard. In the earlier minutes of the residents' committee, however, there are instances where it was entered as 'Louis-bourg,' the old French form, and again as 'Louis-burgh.' In his original title abstracts, N. I. Bowditch once or twice introduced the novel style of 'Lewisbury,' though in one of these instances he used the usual and official form of 'Louisburg' in another place on the same page. It is impossible to determine whether or not these were contemporary entries.

[1] Pepperell Papers, Mass. Hist. Soc., vol. 10, 6th Series, Appendix, pp. 497–563.

LOUISBURG SQUARE

Although correct orthography demands the French spelling of the name, no Hillite would presume to speak it otherwise than after the Yankee Provincial manner of 'Lewisberg.'

XIV
BUILDING–COSTS IN THE THIRTIES

AFTER the deaths of Madam Swan and Benjamin Joy, their executors proceeded to put their Mount Vernon lots on the market. The Joy land, immediately west of the Mason mansion, was sold at public auction in the fall of 1830, Phineas Upham being the purchaser. Two years later, Upham bought the larger portion of the Swan land adjoining, all in fact except a strip next to the Otis place which had a frontage of only eight feet six inches, but widened toward the rear and extended along Pinckney Street from 'Shinbone Alley' and including Numbers 48 to 56 on the street. This last-mentioned fragment was sold to William Sawyer, who lived in the Higginson house, 87 Mount Vernon Street, which he had bought in 1816 after adverse foreign voyages had forced its original owner to liquidate.

Within a few months after his purchase of the Joy land, Upham sold the western half to David Greenough, and both at once began the erection of houses. The houses built by Upham at Numbers 69 and 71 seem to have been the first to be completed in that block, these being sold to Henry Upham and Edmund Baylies on October 19, 1831.

The other houses in that block were built before the end of 1834, Samuel C. Gray buying Number 75, Benjamin Bangs 77, Henry G. Rice 79, which, however, he soon after sold to the Reverend John Turner Sargent, trustee for one of Mrs. Swan's daughters, Christiana R. Richmond, and 81 being bought by John D. Bates. Rice and Bangs built their own houses. The Reverend William Ellery Channing took possession of Number 83 in the summer of 1834. Mr. Channing's house site included the gore on Mount Vernon Street, eight feet six inches wide, the rest of the lot being taken from the easterly side of the old Otis place, Number 85. Greenough and Sawyer sold off the Pinckney Street ends of those lots during the same period. It is interesting to note that the lots fronting on Mount Vernon Street sold at that time for about five thousand dollars. In those cases where houses had been built, the prices ranged from eleven thousand to fourteen thousand dollars. The price paid for the raw land by the developers was not far from sixty cents a square foot. The prices realized by their sales amounted to between two and three dollars a foot. Several of the building contracts are recorded in the Registry. These documents are immensely interesting, but it amazes one in these days to realize that there ever was a time when any kind of a four-story brick house could be built for seventy-five hundred dollars. To be sure, there were no heating plants, other than open grates and fireplaces, and plumbing, in those rare cases where anything of the nature existed, was simple, while the water supply consisted of wells, often shared in common by two or more houses, supplemented by rain cisterns. Sanitation was commonly represented by vaults in the back yards. Flush closets were in use to some extent, in the early twenties at least, but do not appear to have been specified in this instance. In some respects life was more primitive in Boston a little less than a century ago.

Although the figure of seventy-five hundred dollars seems extraordinarily low, yet it must be accepted as correct if any dependence can be placed in the very explicit terms of two building contracts recorded with Suffolk Deeds (L. 358, f. 77 *et seq.*). And there are also the original receipts of the contractors with their signatures, written upon the margins of the records, stating that full satisfaction had been received. No bonuses or additional payments are mentioned, so it is natural to presume that the figures named in the contracts represented the full amount paid.

That these were in no sense mean houses is abundantly proved by their condition after the passage of ninety years. Four houses in a block were built at one time for three individuals. The contracts referred to covered two of these, and presumably the others were duplications, though the contract in that case has not been discovered. The contractors were Francis L. Bates, bricklayer, who lived on the corner of Buttolph (Irving) and May (Revere) Streets, Nathaniel B. Frost, whose name does not appear in the Directory of the period, and Josiah Brown and Richard Emerson, housewrights, of 73 Pond (Bedford) Street. The owners in the case were Phineas Upham, Benjamin Bangs, and Henry G. Rice, and the contracts quoted were for the houses of the last two named.

During the previous year a house had been built next to the Jonathan Mason mansion-house lot for Henry Upham, and in the Bangs and Rice contracts it was specified that their houses should be equal to that one in quality of materials and in the main like it in details. These houses were twenty-seven feet wide by forty-four feet deep with 'swelled fronts.' The contracts required that all materials should be furnished by the contractors, 'not even excepting grates and bells.' 'Grates' in this case meant fireplaces fitted for burning cannel coal. The houses were to be four stories above the cellars, and their basements are high with hammered stone foundations and front steps, iron railings and iron balconies. But the contract did not stop with the houses themselves, but included the laying of edgestones and sidewalks, grading the front yards, which are thirty feet deep, setting a hammered stone wall along the yard fronts with ornamental iron railings on top, paving the back yards with brick and enclosing them with eight-foot high brick walls, building outhouses, cisterns, cesspools and drains, in short providing a thoroughly equipped house and grounds, and all for seventy-five hundred dollars. The houses built on the Mason land four or five years later were larger and somewhat more elaborate in finish, and cost, as some of the contracts show, in the vicinity of seventeen thousand dollars.

Jonathan Mason lived long enough to see this change inaugurated in his neighborhood and to serve a legal notice upon Upham that he was not to assume any right to permanent air and light for the benefit of his new brick house because of the then open area around Mason's mansion next door. William Powell Mason, the eldest son, and Colonel David Sears, a son-in-law, were executors of Mr. Mason's will which was probated November 14, 1831. Beyond turning over the houses devised to the children, there was no further change in that property until the spring of 1836. Madam Mason, who held a life interest in the house, having died the previous January, aged seventy-five years, the great house was then torn down and its site divided into five building lots which were sold at public auction in May of that year. Adam Wallace Thaxter, the mathematical instrument maker,

55, 57, AND 59 MOUNT VERNON STREET

No. 55 at right with front facing down the street; No. 57 set back; No. 59 at
left with Ionic columns

bought Number 59, Jonathan Phillips 61, William Sawyer 63, Jonathan Mason, the second son, who had sold 51, devised to him, took 65, and Abraham T. Lowe became owner of 67. The following year houses began to go up on these lots, Thaxter's recorded contract with the builders being dated March 10, 1837 (L. 417, f. 95), the stipulated figures amounting to seventeen thousand dollars. W. P. Mason bought the lot sold to Sawyer and lived there until his death in 1871, when his heirs sold the house to William Claflin, then Governor of the Commonwealth. It was at this house that the Massachusetts Society for the University Education of Women was organized in 1877. All these properties ran through to Pinckney Street. They sold for upward of three dollars a square foot.

At one time and another that range of houses on the north side of Mount Vernon Street has been the home of many distinguished families. Beside the Honorable Jonathan Mason and Governor Claflin, who lived on the Mason mansion-house property, Senator Henry Cabot Lodge was for some time owner of Number 65, and the Honorable Henry L. Pierce at one time lived at Number 59 which was later the home of Thomas Bailey Aldrich. The Parkman house, Number 57, was long the home of the Honorable Charles Francis Adams the elder, Minister to England during the Civil War and for three years thereafter. At

Number 79 lived Horace Gray, for ten years Chief Justice of the Superior Court of the Commonwealth, and later a Justice of the United States Supreme Court for twenty years. The Reverend William Ellery Channing, of the Arlington Street Church, has already been mentioned as living at Number 83, and the Honorable Harrison Gray Otis at Number 85. Stephen Higginson, Jr., who built Number 87, later Bursar of Harvard College, was the father of Colonel Thomas Wentworth Higginson, and in this house lived for many years General Charles J. Paine, widely known as a managing owner of several yachts built for the defense of the America's Cup. Many others, prominent in the financial and commercial life of Boston, have also lived in that distinguished neighborhood. Daniel Webster lived at Number 57, then known as '8 Mount Vernon, Olive Street,' as a tenant of Mr. Mason, from 1817 to 1819. In the latter year he moved to Somerset Street and the Reverend Sereno Dwight, of Park Street Church, took the Mount Vernon Street house.

XV

THE NORTH SLOPE, VILLAGE

LONG before the Mount Vernon Proprietors began their development of the south-westerly slopes of the Hill, indeed before any of those gentlemen were born, a considerable section on the northwest side had been laid out in streets and house lots. The first attempt to open the extreme westerly pastures to building was made about 1725 by James Allen, a grandson of the Reverend James, who had inherited the north-erly portion of the Allen lot lying between Myrtle and Cambridge Streets. Through this land he cut Grove, Anderson, Garden, Phillips, and Revere Streets and divided the intervening blocks into eighty-nine house lots, each approximately four thousand square feet in area.[1] Shortly thereafter, or about 1729, Byfield Lynde, who had inherited the Zachariah Phillips pasture along the river front, it having come down to him from his grand-father who bought of Phillips in 1672, laid out that tract for building purposes. He continued Phillips and Revere Streets (then called Southack and May) from Allen's boundary across his land, and ex-tended the former so as to swing around on the

[1] Bowditch Abstracts, plan, vol. 5, p. 330.

westerly side of the lot, more or less on the lines of West Cedar Street.[1] His lots, fifty-nine in number, varied considerably in area, especially those lying southerly of what is now Pinckney Street. It was over those southerly lots that the prolonged legal battle raged between the Overseers of the Poor and the Mount Vernon Proprietors between 1836 and 1840, and finally settled out of court in favor of the defendants and without costs.[2]

After another five years, or in 1734, Thomas Buttolph's grandchildren began the development of their pasture, which lay next east of Allen's, and extended along Cambridge Street as far as Hancock, running up the Hill to the south side of Myrtle. Elsewhere it has been seen that Abigail Buttolph, wife of Joseph Belknap, Jr., and her sister Mary, wife of Robert Guttridge, who had inherited the easterly two thirds of the property, cut Joy Street in 1734, calling it Belknap Lane. About the same time their brother, Nicholas Buttolph, to whom had fallen the westerly end of the land, opened Irving Street, to which he gave the family name. Subsequently his heirs laid out that portion of Myrtle Street between Irving and Hancock Streets, also South Russell Street.

Joshua Scottow's pasture, extending from Hancock to just east of Temple Street, came into the

[1] Bowditch Abstracts, plan, vol. 5, p. 68.
[2] Otis Papers; also Overseers' Records, April 1, 1840.

possession of Stephen Minot and Isaiah Tay in 1691. Minot died in 1732, and his heirs shortly thereafter sold lots along the east side of Hancock, then known as George Street, which dates back to that time. Tay died two years before Minot, but his heirs did not begin to cut up their land until 1737, at which time Temple Street was put through under the name of Tay. Between the Minot and Tay pieces was a narrow strip that Minot sold in his lifetime to Samuel Waldo as a ropewalk site, and this in 1769 came into the possession of Joseph Ridgway, from whom the present lane, which bounded the ropewalk on the west, takes its name. In 1727 the Middlecott family laid out Bowdoin Street, but under their patronymic, and beyond this was the narrow strip owned by the Bulfinch family, which extended from Bowdoin Square to Ashburton Place. These two lots, both used as pastures, except for their northern frontages, until after the Revolution, abutted upon a section that had been built upon very early in the town's history. They were on the border-line between town and country.

None of these real estate developments appear to have met with much success. There was some building on the Phillips and Allen lands before the Revolution, but it was of a cheap nature, and populated by a mixed and more or less questionable sort of people. In fact, Bowditch referred to

215

portions of this neighborhood as having been 'the Five Points of Boston until the first Mayor Quincy purged it with his official broom between 1823 and 1828.' Long prior to that, however, a better class of people had been gradually coming in on the north side. Mechanics of all sorts, attracted by the period of good times and the attending building boom in the seventeen-nineties, began to drift into town from the country, and many of these men bought house lots on which to build homes for themselves, and some even built on speculation. Not a few of these seem to have had the real estate sense and made comfortable fortunes, which, in some instances, are not only intact to-day, but have been increased in the hands of their descendants.

Of the original houses on that side of the Hill, those dating back to Revolutionary times or before, none remain to-day, and there are but few now that can claim to have seen any part of the eighteenth century. The story of these ancients is the subject of another chapter. Down to within perhaps twenty years or less a good many small frame dwellings could be found on portions of the Phillips, Allen, and Buttolph lands, that had been built between 1790 and 1810. Some of these were very tidy, suburban-looking structures, sometimes set back from the street with little grassy and flower-decked yards protected behind neat wooden fences. One of the finest specimens of this type stood until quite recent years at the corner of Myrtle and Anderson Streets. A change in population, and a demand for low-priced apartments, brought on a new building boom in which these old-timers have been obliterated.

The local assessment records and the returns of the federal dwellings tax of 1798 have been searched in connection with the titles of the few remaining older appearing houses, to determine if possible the years when they were erected. From the quotations already made from the Taking Books of the local assessors, it has been seen that entries are often found minuting So-and-So's 'New House,' 'House Unfinished,' even specifying in some cases that the house is 'elegant' or 'neat.' But in the earlier years houses were not numbered, and frequently the streets were not named in the record books. In some instances, where a street name was given, houses were assessed under the name of a street that was a whole block away from the actual known location. Much cross-referencing and careful study of this data must, therefore, be made before a definite conclusion can be reached as to any given house. In some instances, before it is possible to understand the assessment records, it becomes necessary to plot an entire block or two, dividing it into house lots in accordance with the deed descriptions and noting the names of the early owners on the various pieces. This, it will be readily understood, is slow and sometimes perplexing, but in most cases it serves to fix the facts.

At the upper end of Pinckney Street, close to Joy Street, there is a small wooden house, now Numbers 5 and 7, that is interesting for several reasons. In the first place, it is one of the most picturesque of the remaining old dwellings on the Hill, and therefore attracts much attention. Many have been the speculations as to its age. Its title is one of the most ancient, and by the same token one of the most puzzling. For that reason alone it may be of some interest to attempt its unraveling here as an illustration of what an antiquary looks upon as a deeply fascinating problem. It was apparent at the outset that this case would develop unusual perplexities, and it became necessary to go back almost two hundred years, to the time when this was a part of Elisha Cooke's two-and-a-half-acre pasture, and to lay down on paper the several house lots into which he and his heirs divided it under sundry deeds beginning in 1735.

Shortly before his death, Cooke began selling this land in small lots fronting on Hancock, Mount Vernon, and Joy Streets. In this way he disposed of several pieces facing east on Joy (then Clapboard) between Mount Vernon (Olive) and Myrtle Streets. The latter street did not then exist. These lots varied from twenty-five to thirty feet wide on Clapboard Street, and extended west seventy-seven feet to the Allen pasture, the old Humphrey Davie orchard lot. According to the designations in the deeds, the purchasers were mainly mechanics of various kinds and seamen. One of the earliest of these sales was made to Temple Decoster, housewright, a lot twenty-five by seventy-seven feet for one hundred pounds public bills of credit. That was in October, 1735. Decoster held the lot until October, 1742, when he sold to John Holliman of Salem, mason and painter, the price being one hundred pounds Provincial bills, old tenor. But Holliman mortgaged back to Decoster for a like sum, and it seems probable that the latter foreclosed, for at his death in 1771 the lot was a part of his estate. His son-in-law, John Hooper, mariner, in conjunction with his wife and her sister, the widow of James Barrett, held the land until the fall of 1786, when they sold to George Middleton and Louis Glapion for thirty pounds.

From the census of 1790 and from various tax records it is learned that Glapion was a mulatto barber, and that Middleton was a 'blackman' who was variously rated as 'drives for Dr. Lloyd' — that is, coachman; as 'jockey,' and as 'horse-breaker.' Only two or three years before their purchase of this land, Jonathan and Benjamin

Austin and Joseph Carnes had bought a strip along the south side of Myrtle Street on which they built two ropewalks, or perhaps enlarged the John Daniel works established there in 1736. Then, in 1792, George and Peter Cade bought another strip along that frontage and built a third ropewalk. These ropewalks extended from Hancock Street to a point west of Grove Street. In 1805, all were bought by Samuel Hammond, Samuel Swett, and Ebenezer Farley, who had associated themselves for the purpose of developing the land for dwellings.

So far as can be ascertained, none of the other lots in the Cooke pasture along Clapboard Street had been built upon when Middleton and Glapion came into the neighborhood. All the lots on both sides of them, together with the Humphrey Davie lot on the west, had already been picked up by Enoch Brown on speculation, as has been stated in another chapter, and these were sold to the Mount Vernon Proprietors by the Brown heirs in 1797. At first these two colored men held their lot in common. Just when they built upon it has not been determined. The earliest assessment found is for 1790, when the valuation of their real estate was entered as twenty-five dollars. This nominal valuation continues for several years, and it might be assumed that it was for vacant land but for the fact that in 1791 a random note appears on a flyleaf of the assessors' Taking Book which reads

MIDDLETON AND GLAPION HOUSE, 5 AND 7
PINCKNEY STREET

Date uncertain

THE PATRIARCHS, 44 AND 46 TEMPLE STREET

Built by Bela Clap about 1787

THE NORTH SLOPE VILLAGE

'Middleton, Lewis Lapier, small house by south side ropewalk.' In the Directories and in the assessors' records the name of the barber appears variously as 'Lapean,' 'Lapier' and 'Glapion.' In the assessment book of 1799 it is entered that he was French and a mulatto. Was he originally from the French West Indies, and was he originally known as 'La Pierre'? When he made a signature he wrote it 'Glapion.'

The following year each was assessed for half a house, and at the same time a deed is found on record in which they agreed to divide the property, which is described as 'a certain tenement and messuage of land.' By that instrument Glapion was given a portion of the house '17 feet 9 inches in length and 15 feet 6 inches in breadth,' beginning at its southwest corner, together with a piece of land adjoining bounding on 'a board fence' twenty-five feet westerly, and twenty-one feet southerly and northerly, also on fences. The dimensions of Middleton's portion of the house are not given, but, from the fact that it was referred to as his 'moiety,' the inference is that they made an even break. Middleton's land area, likewise bounded on board fences, was of equal size with that of his partner, the twenty-five-foot side facing easterly. Judging from the recorded deed, both men signed this document without making a 'mark,' which is suggestive of their ability to read and write. No reference was made to wives, nor was it stated that they were unmarried, but this might be taken for granted, perhaps, owing to the absence of any dower-right releases. That is not conclusive, however, so far as Glapion is concerned, for some years later, when he mortgaged his portion, although certainly married at the time, his wife was not included in the transaction, which led to a complication for the mortgagee, who was eventually obliged to foreclose.

Strangely enough, that deed of division did not mention Clapboard Street as a boundary, but from the fact that Glapion's twenty-five-foot side was bounded westerly, and Middleton's side of similar dimension easterly, it seems fair to assume that the latter had the Clapboard Street end of house and lot, and that the house stood more or less in the middle of the seventy-seven-foot dimension of the land, and close up against what is now the Pinckney Street frontage. Pinckney Street was not thought of in 1792, and was not laid out until nearly ten years later when the Mount Vernon Proprietors began selling lots on its north side. What constitutes the 'length' or 'breadth' of a house is an arbitrary matter, but, in order to make this divided property measure up to twenty-five by seventy-seven feet, it becomes necessary to assume that in this case seventeen feet nine inches in length meant east and west along Pinckney

Street. If that was half of a house fifteen feet six inches in breadth, with a lot of land on each end twenty-one feet long by twenty-five wide, the required area is fully satisfied with a wee bit to spare.

When that United States tax was levied in 1798 against every dwelling-house in the country, together with the land adjacent up to two acres in extent, in order to raise two million dollars for the Federal Treasury, this property was rated as 'a wooden dwelling, east on Clapboard Street, south on Jonathan Mason and Harrison Gray Otis [that is, the Mount Vernon Proprietors], land 1925 square feet, house 345 square feet, one story, four windows, value $600.' The town of Boston's assessors valued it at one hundred dollars that same year. The area of the land is the correct figure for a lot twenty-five by seventy-seven, but the size of the house is not the square of thirty-five feet six inches by fifteen feet six inches. It is two hundred and five square feet less, in fact. Were this the only puzzling feature in the problem, it might be brushed aside as a possible clerical error, but as time goes on, and mortgages, probate settlements, and sales multiply, the difficulties deepen. Some of these formalities introduce new descriptions quite as vague as the foregoing.

In the spring of 1804, Glapion needed a little ready cash for some purpose and mortgaged his portion of the property, presumably the western half of the whole lot, to Benjamin Russell, who, in the previous year, had bought a lot next to Glapion on Pinckney Street. Mr. Russell was editor and publisher of the 'Columbian Centinel.' The sum loaned, according to the deed, was $52.75. This was discharged in September, 1811, but on the same day Glapion gave to Russell another mortgage deed to secure a new loan, this time $946. In each of these instances the deed description follows that in the deed of division quoted above. It was in this connection that Lucy, the wife of Louis, was not brought in to release her right of dower. It might be a reasonable assumption that this money was borrowed for the purpose of making improvements upon the house, but there is nothing in the assessment rolls to encourage that conclusion. In 1801, Middleton was assessed 'for small house $100,' and Glapion for a 'long room and shop $200.' Two years later the combined tax value increased to thirteen hundred dollars which was a year before the date of the first small mortgage, and that proves nothing one way or another, because a year later still the valuation dropped to eight hundred dollars, and during the next ten years it varied all the way from that to twelve hundred dollars and back again to eight hundred dollars.

In the assessors' Street Book of 1811 it was

entered that both Middleton and Glapion were old men. Three years later, Glapion died and his will, which was executed October 19, 1813, was probated June 13, 1814. Lucy was named as executrix and sole heir to all property, real and personal, which consisted of the house and land, appraised at seven hundred dollars, and sundry items of furniture, which included one bed and bedding, four chairs, two tables, and a pair of iron fire-dogs, also his 'razors and barber tools' and a glass case, all valued at twenty-four dollars. When the funeral expenses were paid, including a charge for two pounds of candles for the church, the executrix had a ruinous red-ink balance on her account, and in January, 1815, she went into voluntary insolvency. That spring Middleton died leaving all his property to his 'good friend Tristram Babcock, of Boston, mariner.' His will was dated April 3, 1815, and probated April 17th. This document he signed with his mark, perhaps being too ill to undertake a signature. The inventory rated his 'House and land in Pinckney Street' at $770, and his furniture and numerous and varied sundries amounted to $50.95. His furnishings consisted of a feather bed, an under-bed and two blankets, two bedsteads, five old chairs, a maple dining-table, and three pine tables, two iron kettles, 'both broken,' a tin kitchen, and a rat trap. There were also various odds and ends of carpenter's and gardener's tools and such items connected with his trade of jockey and horse-breaker as a saddle and four bridles, a halter and bits of harness. There were also a musket and a violin.

Lucy evidently left after her husband's death, for that spring the assessors noted in their Taking Book that the portion owned by the 'heirs of Glapion' was an 'empty house.' The insolvency proceedings in Lucy's case did not begin until the autumn following Middleton's death and these led to an action in the Court of Common Pleas, brought by the mortgagee, Russell, to secure possession of the Glapion portion of the house. A judgment was rendered in his favor in October, subject, however, to his acknowledgement of the widow's dower rights. This he recognized in a deed to her in which he quotes the report of the two referees appointed by the court to set off the dower. They described the whole lot as thirty-seven feet on Pinckney Street, and twenty-six feet wide, which is one foot nine inches shorter on Pinckney Street, and one foot wider than was called for in the division deed. But then they go on to describe the premises more in detail, and especially that part of the house itself which is to be the widow's portion. This, it was stated, began at the southeast corner of the house, ran twelve feet six inches on Pinckney Street, then turned at right angles 'through said dwelling house' to the rear of the lot, twelve feet six inches, easterly there, and twenty-six feet southerly to the street. She was also given the use of the cellar under her end, but the land adjoining was not mentioned. Obviously this is the easterly portion of the house, which supposedly had been Middleton's end under their partition. Lucy accepted this settlement by making her mark upon the document. That she then returned to the house is evident, for she was assessed there the following year and her name appears also in the Directory for 1816, though as 'Lucy Lapean, Pinckney Street.' With the exception of two years she was assessed there constantly through 1832.

Soon after Babcock took possession of Middleton's portion, he mortgaged the property twice for small sums, and then, on January 2, 1817, sold to David Shillaber for five hundred dollars. In each of these transactions the property is described as two pieces of land with buildings on Pinckney and Belknap Streets, 'which premises are the easterly and westerly division made between Louis Glapion and George Middleton, March 24, 1792.' That masterpiece of legal indefiniteness is sufficient to warrant the inference that Middleton had somehow secured title to Glapion's bit of land adjacent to the house. Possibly Glapion had deeded it to him with the consent of the mortgagee and the instrument was never sent to record. Perhaps it was under that deed that Middleton and Glapion swapped sides in the house. Meantime the Middleton side had been rented to Michael Riley, truckman, later on constable, and one of Babcock's mortgage deeds recited that the property was then 'occupied and improved by Michael Riley.' 'Improved' was here used in the sense that Riley made use of the property, which was in accordance with an ancient legal usage of the verb. The Riley family continued to live there for some years, as did Lucy in the other half. In 1823, a new complication entered the record when, David Shillaber having died, his estate was appraised and divided in the Probate Office. Under that division there was assigned to the son, Daniel Shillaber, a 'tenement situate on Pinckney Street and the land thereto belonging, bounded easterly on land formerly owned by Louis Glapion, there measuring 25 feet, southerly on Pinckney Street, there measuring 21 feet, westerly on land belonging to Benjamin Russell, there measuring 25 feet.'

This is plainly enough that plot of ground supposedly set off to Glapion on the west of the house in the original division, but how about the 'tenement'? Hitherto this description had covered a piece of vacant land bounded by board fences. A little further search of the titles reveals the fact that in April, 1824, Russell decided that he wanted to build the two brick houses now Numbers 9 and

11 Pinckney Street, but his lot was not sufficiently wide for the purpose. He therefore bought of Shillaber the land next to him, which, by the way, shrank a foot under this deed and became twenty feet on the street side. A 'shop standing on the premises' was included in this sale. It will be recalled that in 1801 Glapion was assessed for 'a long room and a shop.' It should not be assumed, however, that this was what the appraisers of the David Shillaber estate termed a 'tenement.' The conclusion that Glapion owned the west end of the lot in the beginning would seem to be confirmed by this, but reading further in that same deed the statement is found that this is 'the same estate which was formerly George Middleton's and which he devised to Tristram Babcock, which said Babcock conveyed to David Shillaber and which was assigned to me [that is, Daniel Shillaber] in the division of said David's estate.' All of which is most confusing unless it is accepted as a confirmation of that other assumption that Glapion and Middleton swapped property at some time and in some unrecorded fashion.

On that same day in April, 1824, when Russell bought of Shillaber, the latter bought from the former 'a piece of land southerly on Pinckney Street 38 ft. 9 in., westerly on said Daniel's [Shillaber's] 25 ft. northerly on Russell 38 ft. 9 in. [he had bought the lot behind and facing Joy

Street], easterly on land assigned to the widow of David Shillaber as part of her dower 25 ft., with the buildings.' It further states that a part of the premises conveyed are subject to a life estate of Lucy Glapion, widow, as deeded to Russell in Glapion's mortgage of 1811 and by Russell to Lucy to satisfy her dower claims in 1815. Here is a return to the frontage measurement of thirty-eight feet nine inches, which seemed to have been implied in the old Middleton-Glapion division, but which was cut to thirty-seven feet when Russell deeded the dower to Lucy. This also seems to locate Lucy in the easterly side of the house.

Mr. Shillaber is thus clearly left with a piece of property lying between the land and shop that he sold to Russell and this domicile of Lucy's. If the piece he sold to Russell was twenty feet, and the piece he bought of Russell was thirty-eight feet nine inches on the street, this intermediate parcel must have been eighteen feet three inches in order to make good the demanded seventy-seven feet of frontage. This must have been the westerly portion of the house as bought from Middleton's heir by the elder Shillaber, and is probably the 'tenement' mentioned by the appraisers of his estate. Apparently they described the adjacent lot with the shop by metes and bounds, but contented themselves with this simple designation for the house. The only discovered recorded interest of Mrs. David Shillaber in any part of this property is found in the tax rolls, where, after 1823, she is assessed for a building, apparently rented at that time as a tenement, but later as a shop, on the corner of Joy Street. Russell's deed to Mrs. Shillaber's son of the thirty-eight feet nine inches must have included this. Why he should have done this if he did not own it is a mystery, but it is equally mysterious how the Shillaber family came to possess it, inasmuch as this land, and the portion of the house in which Mrs. Glapion lived, were adjudged Russell's by the Court of Common Pleas nine years before, subject only to Lucy's right of domicile in the house itself.

None of these things are of any material importance at the present day to any one for any purpose, since on January 1, 1833, Daniel Shillaber paid Lucy Glapion $416.66 for her rights. Moreover, whatever Madam Shillaber's rights were, they have been fully satisfied, lo these many years, for the property has never been out of the family, and they have even bought back that portion sold to Russell in 1824, together with the rest of his lot and the two houses that he built. By inference and elimination it is concluded that the Joy Street corner lot was the one now covered by a frame building which houses a store and a restaurant, and that the brick dwelling, now numbered

3 Pinckney Street, was built by Daniel Shillaber in 1833 on the site formerly occupied by Lucy Glapion. At all events, the tax records show that he was 'erecting' a building that year which was obviously located between the store on the corner and the present double-numbered house, which had then been occupied for several years by two shoemakers. William Younger had his home and shop there in 1827 and 1828, and in 1831 he was succeeded by Alexander H. Clapp.

By the courtesy of the owners and of the occupant of the older dwelling, the house has been examined from cellar to rooftree, and the whole property has been measured inside and out. The only modern measurement that tallies satisfactorily with those given in the legal papers is the thirty-eight feet, nine inches, of frontage westerly from Joy Street. That point is the party wall between the brick house of 1833 and the older house numbered 5 and 7. The latter is twenty-one feet four inches on Pinckney Street by eighteen feet four inches deep, which figures do not in the least agree with any of the ancient house measurements. By adding those frontages together, it is seen that the western wall of the old house is all but sixty feet from Joy Street, so that if Russell actually bought twenty feet from that end of the old lot it must have been nearer eighty feet long than seventy-seven originally.

THE NORTH SLOPE VILLAGE

While it is not at all likely that the old house is the original structure built by Middleton and Glapion shortly after their purchase of the land in 1786, there are two things about it that brand it as an antique; namely, its timbering and its chimney, the latter with deep old-fashioned fireplaces. It must be all of a century old, and it has every appearance of even greater antiquity. Hales's map of 1814 shows buildings on this site extending from Joy Street to within about twenty feet of the Russell lot. It also shows what was probably the shop on the western end. There is small wonder, perhaps, that the house should wear an aspect of venerability after passing through such a series of experiences as have been noted here.

It has been shown in a previous chapter that on the opposite side of Pinckney Street a good brick house had been built by Stephen Higginson, Jr., on the corner of Joy, with three stables next to it, in 1803, and that a little farther down the street several other brick houses had been built between 1827 and 1830. The north side of Pinckney Street had been pretty well built up from Joy to Anderson Streets between 1801 and 1806, and many of those old houses still stand, and are but little if any changed in outward appearance. Some of the earlier ones were frame structures or combinations of brick and wood, and some of them remain in slightly altered form. Susanna Benjamin,

233

later Mrs. Ebenezer Weld, was assessed in 1801 for a 'neat new house side rope walk.' This was Number 21, which was sold to William Whitwell in 1824 and altered somewhat by him. Joseph Batson, a plasterer, and James Otis, carpenter, were assessed in 1801 each for an 'elegant house unfinished.' These men owned the sites of the present houses numbered from 13 to 21 Pinckney, a span now representing both ancient and modern houses. Farther along toward Anderson Street Numbers 47 and 49 were built in 1804 by Jeremiah Gardner, carpenter, and Peter Osgood, bricklayer. It has already been noted that Gardner built a number of good houses on the Hill on speculation at about that time. These two were among the best, and Number 47 retains all of its original features. It was sold in 1805 to Isaac Scholfield, dealer in what was known as English goods. An elderly lady who died there within recent years was fond of telling how, in her girlhood, before the houses were built on the opposite side of the street and on Mount Vernon Street beyond, she could see the trees on the Common from the upper windows of this Scholfield house in which she grew up.

Mr. Clapp, the shoemaker, occupied the double-numbered house on the Middleton-Glapion site from 1831 to 1839. In the latter year Joseph K. Adams rented the house and moved there with his bride. He also was a custom boot and shoemaker who, in the course of his fifty years or more of active life, established a high reputation. He is said to have been particularly successful in affording relief to customers suffering with broken arches, and enjoyed the confidence of leading physicians who advised patients thus afflicted to try Mr. Adams's boots. His shop was in the western end of the house, and the shop entrance was Number 7, now long disused. The Adams family, which eventually included several children, lived there until 1892. Number 9, one of the Russell houses, was for five years, in 1836 and 1841, the home of Lowell Mason, the musical composer. Number 11 was long the residence of Edwin P. Whipple, essayist, critic, and lecturer, and for the past twenty years has been the home of Miss Alice Brown, novelist. Maturin M. Ballou, editor of 'Gleason's Pictorial,' later 'Ballou's Monthly,' and at one time of the 'Boston Globe,' lived at Number 15 in the first year of his married life, 1847. At that time this house was the easterly counterpart of the brick and wood house now Number 17, and faced east on a side yard adorned with apple trees. It was in this house, also, that Elizabeth Peabody had her kindergarten, the second established in this country, between 1860 and 1867.

XVI

THE OLDEST OF THEM ALL

IN the absence of any positive proof as to the date of the oldest house on the Middleton and Glapion Pinckney Street lot, it must yield to others, with abundant recorded facts behind them, the claim to being the oldest unmodified dwellings on any part of the Hill. A careful search up and down all the older streets, with excursions into every alley and court, with a view to locating any house that might show signs of considerable antiquity, netted a total of four that warranted an investigation of their titles. Two of these, twin houses in Temple Street, seem to be fully entitled to the distinction of being rated as the oldest by ten or perhaps a dozen years of any now standing. Next to these ranks a brick house on South Russell Street. The fourth house investigated is a frame dwelling on Smith's Court, off Joy Street, which looks older than it really is. The latter began its existence, however, nearly or quite a century and a quarter ago, which fully entitles it to a place in these pages. There is another old-appearing house in the rear of Joy Street, near Myrtle, but its record is complicated and uncertain.

The Temple Street houses, Numbers 44 and 46,

now the clergy houses connected with Saint John's Church on Bowdoin Street, stand on a part of the Joshua Scottow pasture that came into the possession of the heirs of Isaiah Tay, who laid out the street in 1737 as Tay Street. In 1769, it was renamed Temple Street in honor of Lady Temple, a daughter of James Bowdoin. Robert Pierpont, of Roxbury, a member of the family from which J. Pierpont Morgan, of New York, is descended, became the owner of the southerly end of the Tay land, and in 1785 he deeded a strip two hundred and twenty-one feet in length on the east side of the street to Thomas Parker and others for eighteen pounds in bills of the Commonwealth. In this deed he certified that 'the said sum' had been paid to him eleven years previously by Parker. The new owners immediately conveyed a piece of this land, fifty-one feet wide on Temple Street, to Bela Clap, housewright, for fifty-five pounds lawful money. From an investigation of the title and the tax records it is evident that this land was the site of 44 and 46 Temple Street.

From outward appearances one would say that these houses were probably built by one man, or at least at one and the same time from identical plans. The records, however, seem to indicate that Number 44 was built first, though this has not been established with sufficient definiteness to warrant a positive statement to that effect. The tax books of that period are incomplete, and the entries are not as detailed and precise as they were a few years later.

The Taking Book for 1786, the year after Bela Clap bought the land, shows the names of others who had bought lots along that frontage, but Clap's name does not appear among them. The same is true for 1787, but in the Tax Book for that year there are found Bela and Caleb Clap, the former assessed for real estate to the value of one hundred dollars, and both assessed for personalty in the sum of fifty dollars each. The Tax Book for the following year is missing, but both Bela and Caleb are found in the Taking Book, though no valuations are given there.

Meantime, in 1787, Bela Clap sold to Caleb for £27.10.0 a lot twenty-five and a half feet wide on the street and bounded north on Bela's land. In 1789, Bela's name appears in the first Directory, where his address is given as Temple Street. Caleb's name does not figure in the tax lists for 1789, 1790, or 1791, though Bela was assessed in those years in the same location as before. In 1792, the deeds show, however, that Caleb sold to George Homer, merchant, for three hundred pounds, 'a certain dwelling house with the land under the same and thereto belonging' which bounded north on Bela Clap. Thereafter Bela and George Homer are found assessed as living side by side until 1797, when Clap sold his house for three thousand dollars to Thomas Stutson, housewright, the lot bounding south on George Homer. Going back to 1790, and consulting the census of that year, Bela is found in the right position, but no Caleb is mentioned.

Within six months after the purchase of Number 44 by Stutson, he sold to William Hayden, merchant. That was the year when the Federal tax was levied on dwellings, and the records of that assessment show that Hayden and Homer were taxed on adjoining 'three story wooden dwellings,' each valued at sixteen hundred dollars. But Hayden did not hold the property long, for in 1802 he sold for thirty-five hundred dollars to John Hodgkins, mariner, who made this his home for many years. In 1850, after Hodgkins's death, the house was transferred to Isaac Davenport as trustee for the heirs. The Homer family was also long in possession of Number 46. Mr. Homer died in 1837, but the Directory places his widow there through 1844. On her death the house became the property of her daughters, Mrs. Sarah Sumner Carlton and Mrs. Susannah Ridgway Lord, the latter the wife of Melvin Lord, a well-known publisher and bookseller, who lived on Bowdoin Street. Both of these houses originally stood a trifle back from the street, but in 1851 a widening took place which sheared off about three feet from the frontages for street purposes.

The next oldest house is the three-story brick dwelling numbered 43 South Russell Street. This house stands on a portion of the Thomas Buttolph pasture across which a son, Nicholas Buttolph, laid out the present Irving Street in 1733, calling it Buttolph Street. The portion of the old pasture owned by Nicholas extended east to the rear of the houses on the easterly side of South Russell Street, and from Cambridge to Myrtle Street. According to a deed given in 1766 to her sons by Mrs. Knight Leverett, a daughter of Nicholas, South Russell Street was laid out by her husband and her sister's husband, John Phillips, in 1737. The Street Department's historical summary of the streets and alleys gives 1795 as the year in which the name South Russell Street was applied. Until that time, and indeed until 1802 for the most part, as witnessed by numerous deeds of record, it was referred to as 'a new street.' The pasture lay up along the hillside for about six hundred feet above Cambridge Street, and Myrtle Street was laid out along its southerly end. The northerly end, three hundred feet deep, came into the possession of Nathaniel Wheelwright, and in 1790 his administrator sold this to Nathaniel Hurd Furnass. That sale covered the land bounded by Cambridge, Irving, and South Russell Streets, and southerly as far as the lots now numbered 36 Irving and 33 South Russell. The price paid was fifty pounds lawful money.

Only three months later, Furnass found a purchaser in William Breed, baker, who paid ninety-five pounds lawful money. That seems like a large advance in price, but Mr. Breed seems to have anticipated the boom that shortly thereafter affected the entire Hill, for after holding the land four years he sold, in July, 1794, to Appleton Prentiss, paper-stainer, for four hundred pounds lawful money.

Prentiss built a brick and wood house for himself on the corner of Cambridge and South Russell Streets, assessed in 1796 as a 'large new house,' and on the southerly end of the land, on the site of 32 and 34 Irving Street, and probably running through nearly to South Russell Street, he built, what he termed in a mortgage covering the property, 'the paper manufactory.' Meantime, in 1796, Prentiss bought the southerly end of the block through to Myrtle Street from the Leverett heirs and immediately began selling house lots, large and small, fronting on Irving and South Russell Streets. One of these, forty feet wide, and running seventy feet from street to street, was bought by Joseph Ditson, subsequently rated as a trader. This deed was dated April 19, 1797, which date is interesting because of its historic associations, and because of the coincidence that Ditson had just married a Lexington girl, a daughter of Solomon Pierce who was one of the

Minute Men wounded on Lexington Green twenty-two years before. Ditson himself was descended from one of the settlers of Billerica, which endears his memory to the writer whose forebears were members of that little company of pioneers of 1650 on the banks of the 'Shawshin.' The name of Ditson later became well known in Boston through the enterprise of the music publisher, Oliver Ditson, who was the fifth child of this Joseph and Lucy.

Ditson's lot was described as beginning at a point on Irving Street 'ninety-four feet from the building called the callico or paper manufactory,' and since it is known definitely that his lot included what are now 46 and 48 Irving, as well as 43 South Russell Street, this deed makes it possible to locate that factory building quite accurately. Prentiss referred to this industry again in another deed one month later, by which he sold a large lot next north of Ditson's to Elizabeth Fennecy, widow, of Cambridge. A new house was included in this sale and restrictions were imposed to the effect that no buildings or 'close fence' should be built on the northerly end of the property so as to obstruct the light of the windows of the building belonging to 'the callico printing corporation.' That particular lot, being eighty-nine feet wide on the two streets, abutted, therefore, upon the southerly side of this factory, which, as stated above, was on the site of 32 and 34 Irving Street.

BASEMENT KITCHEN OF DITSON HOUSE

43 SOUTH RUSSELL STREET, BUILT BY OLIVER
DITSON'S FATHER ABOUT 1797

THE OLDEST OF THEM ALL

THE OLDEST OF THEM ALL

Ditson paid fourteen cents a foot for his land. Evidently he built a frame house at once on the Irving Street side, for in less than a month after his purchase he sold a half-interest in the whole lot, also three-eighths of a lot and 'one-half of the west end of a wooden house,' to Jonas Twist. Possibly this may be taken to indicate that they built that house in partnership. Not one of the foregoing deeds went to record until February, 1801, at which time Ditson is found mortgaging a brick house which obviously was located on the South Russell Street side of his land. A search of the town tax records failed to reveal when this brick house, now 43 South Russell Street, was built. In 1798, for instance, Jonas Twist was not found, but there was a Solomon Twist 'toleman on the bridge' (that is, tollgate-tender on the West Boston Bridge to Cambridge), and the next name in the enumeration is that of Joseph Ditson, both on Buttolph Street, but neither was assessed for real estate. Not until 1801 is any evidence found in that source that any Twist or Ditson owned real estate. Down to that time they, like many others in that vicinity, were assessed for the number of rooms that they personally occupied. In that year Jonas Twist was assessed on Buttolph Street for real estate valued at one hundred dollars, while Ditson's name appears with the notation that his property was 'taken in next street.' Two pages farther on, but still under the heading of Buttolph Street, which is indicative of the unsystematic manner in which this work was done in those days, Ditson is located with the laconic note, 'Owns the house,' which was valued at two hundred dollars. He was also taxed on one hundred dollars personalty.

In the spring of the following year, Ditson sold a brick house in South Russell Street, the northerly half, twenty feet by thirty-six, to Henry Barge, fisherman, for twelve hundred dollars, and the southerly half of like dimensions to John Chipman, mariner, for eleven hundred and fifty dollars, the entry and stairs in common. Here is conclusive evidence of Ditson's ownership of 43 South Russell Street at that time, but nothing to show that he built it. By turning to the records of the United States tax of October, 1798, however, this entry is found: 'Ditson and Twist, owners and occupiers, brick dwelling, East on —— Street, south on Amidon, north on Carnes, three stories, 1440 feet land, $800.' Another entry is as follows: 'Ditson and Twist, Captain Dunn and others, occupiers, wooden dwelling, west on Buttolph Street, north on Carnes, south on Amidon, two stories, 1440 feet, $1000.' This accounts for the whole lot of forty feet frontage on two streets by seventy feet deep, except that the area as taxed is eighty square feet greater than the supposed extent of the land, also for the wooden house on Irving Street and for the brick house on South Russell, and shows conclusively that both houses were built within the first year or a little more after Ditson bought the land, and certainly by 1798. This fact has been fully checked by a plotting of the block bounded by Cambridge, Irving, Myrtle, and South Russell Streets in accordance with that Federal tax record, each abutting owner mentioned being run down to find the areas assessed. The only discrepancy is found in the statement that Ditson's land bounded north on Carnes, whereas it has been shown that Mrs. Fennecy owned the lot next north of him, and Thomas J. Carnes that north of her. This is accounted for readily enough by a marriage contract, recorded with Suffolk Deeds (L. 190, f. 38), which shows that Mrs. Fennecy married Thomas Jenner Carnes, the rope manufacturer, just prior to this assessment.

This close examination of the tax record is interesting for the reason that it shows how rapidly this block was bought up and built upon after Mr. Prentiss put it on the market. On the Cambridge Street end, which he acquired in 1794, there were two houses of brick and wood, and six wooden houses, presumably in addition to the calico factory which was not included in the tax. On the southerly portion, bought from the Leverett heirs, there were six houses, apparently all of wood except Ditson's three-story brick dwelling, though there was another three-story house on the Irving Street side, the material of which was not specified. This makes a total of fifteen dwellings and the factory, all built within the space of less than four years. At present there are nearly forty houses and a large school on that land. Of the old ones Ditson's three-story brick house alone remains to-day and, thanks to the fact that it came into the possession of an investor whose heirs were never moved to make extensive alterations, it has come down in practically unchanged form.

Down to 1834 the Ditson house continued in divided ownership. Barge, and his widow after him, lived in the north side until 1834, when the family sold out to William Pike, baker, who had owned the south side since 1820. Captain Chipman, who bought the south side from Ditson, lived there until 1810, when he sold to Josiah Wait, trader. Seven years later, Wait sold to Elijah Stedman, a provision dealer on Anderson Street, who sold to Pike. Pike himself seems to have moved to Cambridge Street in 1826, but held the South Russell Street property as an investment until 1855, when it was sold to H. T. Rowell, a Portland Street blacksmith, who lived there until 1857. The next owner was Charles W. Brewster, who was a maker of springs at 55 Sudbury Street, and five years later Brewster sold to Ira Litchfield, housewright. Mr. Litchfield lived at 31 South Russell Street with a shop across the street at Number 16. He bought as an investment, and Mr. Brewster continued to live in the old house as his tenant down to 1875, in which year both Litchfield and Brewster bade good-bye to South Russell Street as a place of residence, the one going to Plymouth, the other to Medford. Number 43 has remained in the Litchfield estate constantly until recently, however, when it was purchased by the present occupant as a residence, and in whose hands its homelike qualities have been restored.

Severely plain outwardly, its interior finish, while not as elaborate as in the more costly houses of its day, presents a fine example of the good taste followed by the housewrights of that period. In the basement is the original kitchen with its old-time cavernous fireplace and oven, a room made doubly picturesque by the heavy hand-hewn and time-stained ceiling timbers. In the early twenties this room may have been the bakery of William Pike. At all events, this was his only address, business or otherwise, according to the Directory, until his removal to Cambridge Street in 1826, and the door leading directly into this room from the street is suggestive of commercial possibilities. The fireplaces, one in every room, had long ago been bricked up and fitted with stove thimbles. When broken open the backs were found to be badly burned, necessitating their replacement. In one room the fireplace was shallower than the rest, but the removal of the back revealed a deeper hearth behind which also gave evidence of having seen many years of service. It is remarkable that a house, held as this one was for half a century or more as an investment property, should have escaped radical alterations within and without. Its preservation is due to its ownership throughout this period by a family of conservative tendencies. In every way the house is a fine model of the moderate-priced substantial dwelling of its day, and under its present ownership the safety of the landmark is assured to the community..

Although the Smith's Court house did not prove to be as old as a first survey indicated possible, it is nevertheless an interesting representative of the north-side settlement. Completely restored by a recent purchaser for his own occupancy, it has become one of the ancient permanent landmarks. This portion of the Buttolph pasture, it will be recalled, was opened up in 1734 by Mrs. Belknap and Mrs. Guttridge when they laid out Belknap Street. Edward Carnes, the ropemaker, bought a good deal of this property, and in June, 1798, Elizabeth (Fennecy) Carnes, widow of Thomas Jenner Carnes, sold a piece of it to William Lancaster and Benajah Brigham, bricklayers, which faced south on a twenty-foot wide passageway for a distance of forty-seven feet, and abutted east on other land of Carnes twenty-nine feet. The following year Jeduthan Wellington, a well-known lawyer of the Belmont family of that name, sold to these same men a piece described as 'part of the estate of Edward Carnes,' twenty-nine feet wide on Belknap Street and, like the former lot, facing south for forty-seven feet on the passageway. That passageway was what came to be known as 'May's Court' in 1812 and later, in 1848, as 'Smith's Court.' Thus Lancaster and Brigham owned a strip twenty-nine feet wide on Joy Street and ninety-four feet on the Court.

The earliest recognizable assessment of this property is found in the Taking Book for 1800, where William Lancaster and Benajah Brigham, masons, are each assessed for three hundred dollars on real estate in that vicinity, with the notation that they are 'in company.' It also is there recorded that these men occupied the 'back end of house.' Taking all these things into consideration, plus the evidence which the structure itself affords to-day in the style of its construction, there is good reason to believe that this house was built not later than that spring, and not impossibly in 1799. Inasmuch as neither Lancaster nor Brigham can be found in the rolls of the Federal tax of 1798, which was taken as of October 1st of that year, it seems clear that 1799 is the earliest date for the building.

In January, 1802, Brigham deeded his half-interest in this property to Lancaster for fifteen hundred dollars, and seven years later the latter sold the easterly half of the house and the thirty-five-foot wide lot east of it and cornering on Joy Street, to Joseph Powers, trader. For the corner lot Powers paid eight hundred dollars and for the half-house, one thousand dollars. In 1814, Powers bought the westerly half of the house from Lancaster for eight hundred dollars, thus coming into possession of the whole lot, twenty-nine by ninety-four, as bought by the two masons from Mrs. Carnes and Squire Wellington. Powers lived there a number of years. Meantime, in 1806, the African Baptist Church Society had bought a lot on the opposite side of the Court and built a brick church. It was in this building that the New England Anti-Slavery Society was born in January, 1832, under the leadership of William Lloyd Garrison. That building still stands exactly as of yore, but it is now a Jewish synagogue.

XVII
SOME ECCENTRICITIES

A SINGULAR title complication was early staged on a portion of the old Allen pasture. This was the land laid out in streets and lots in 1725 by a grandson of the Reverend James Allen, the former owner. Among the early purchasers here was William Bulfinch, who bought, in 1729, a lot on the corner of Anderson and Revere Streets, one hundred feet frontage on the former and forty feet on the latter. The block lying along the north side of Revere Street, between Anderson and Garden Streets, had been divided into five lots, each forty feet wide on Revere Street. Nearly forty years later, in 1766, the two lots next east of Mr. Bulfinch's came into the possession of Henderson Inches. Bowditch referred to this matter briefly in his 'Gleaner' papers, and in his original title abstracts there is further comment upon it. In those days this pasture still remained pretty much in the rough. The streets that had been laid out through it were probably not well defined, and the location of a lot, bought by number from a plan, might not be easy of accomplishment without a resurvey. At all events, Mr. Inches made a slight mistake in locating

the corners of his eighty feet of Revere Street frontage, and set his southwest corner stake seventy
feet east of Anderson, instead of forty feet away
from that corner, as he should have done. This
pushed his double lot over toward Garden Street
so that it lapped thirty feet onto the second lot from
that end of the block. In other words, he enclosed
only ten feet of his own westerly lot, all of his
easterly lot, and thirty feet of the lot next east of
that, which belonged to some one else.

Meantime, Mr. Bulfinch built a house on some
portion of his Anderson Street corner. After his
death his heirs sold this parcel to Harrison Gray
Otis in 1805, who discovered that there was thirty
feet more land between Anderson Street and the
Inches property than he supposed that he had
bought. This matter he seems to have discussed
with the Inches family, for 'Gleaner' stated that
they 'told Mr. Otis that if they ever lost the thirty
feet which had been accidentally enclosed, they
should take this thirty feet adjoining his lot, but
otherwise not.' Mr. Otis, therefore, cut his land
into four lots of twenty-five feet frontage on
Anderson Street by seventy feet on Revere Street,
and these were promptly sold. His purchasers
rearranged the land, however, so as to have three
house lots fronting on Revere Street, and one on
Anderson, behind them. Those Revere Street lots
are now represented by Numbers 33, 35, and 37

on that street, Number 33 being entirely on the disputed thirty feet and some six feet of Number 35.

Peter Osgood and Jonathan Whitney, two brick-masons whose names were later found in connection with the construction of a good many of the best houses on the Hill, bought those Revere Street lots in July, 1806, and presumably built houses there for sale. J. G. Hales's map of 1814 shows two disconnected houses on that land and one on the Inches lot. The map does not clearly show whether they were of brick or wood. In December, 1806, the lot now numbered 33 was sold to Hannah Stevens, widow, for twelve hundred dollars. The tax records show that in 1809 a small house had been built on the Inches land, occupied that year by W. Todd, 'snuff-maker.' In June, 1817, Mrs. Stevens sold her house to Atherton H. Stevens, at that time designated as a mason, though subsequently he appears as a grocer. In 1818, he was taxed there for an unfinished house, and it is assumed that he either altered the old house or built anew at that time. At all events, the present Number 33 Revere Street is the result of Mr. Stevens's work, except that the front door was originally recessed and approached by a flight of steps. The house was sold in August, 1823, to Otis Tileston, described in the deed as a baker, though the Directory shows that he was then a member of the dry-goods firm of Tileston and Wenzel, corner of Court and Washington Streets. Tileston paid two thousand dollars for the property. He had previously bought the lots west to Anderson Street, where, in 1818, he was assessed, like his neighbor Stevens, for an unfinished house. His two houses have been superseded in recent years by apartment buildings.

In all this time no one had disputed the right to the Number 33 lot, and it was not until some ten years later, in 1833, that the question was raised by persons who had bought the two forty-foot lots on the Garden Street end of the block. They discovered that there was only fifty feet of frontage available between the Inches property and Garden Street, instead of the eighty which their deed demanded. An investigation revealed the true situation, and the Inches family was sued for its encroachment. They in turn sued Mr. Otis. Referees settled the case to the mutual satisfaction of all parties, and the Inches heirs, having deeded the extra thirty feet to Mr. Otis, he confirmed the same to his grantees, and the title was finally quieted. Just ten years from that time, in 1843, John W. Rollins, a builder, bought the Inches land and put up four houses on the Revere Street front and six in the rear, facing a quaint little court, since known as 'Rollins Place.'

It was within ten years after Appleton Prentiss began the development of the Irving-South Russell Street block that Messrs. Hammond, Swett, and

SOME ECCENTRICITIES

Farley bought the ropewalks and other property on both sides of Myrtle Street, and for several years following 1805 that section, from Hancock Street to west of Anderson, was the scene of active building. On the southeasterly corner of Myrtle and Anderson Streets stands a four-square brick house, with a deeply recessed front door on the Anderson Street side, which is much admired for its simple dignity. This was one of the earlier houses built on the ropewalk site. William Homer, stonecutter, bought this lot in the fall of 1806 with the restriction that any house built there should be of brick and not less than three stories in height. During the following year Mr. Homer built the present house, which is four stories high, and in June, 1808, sold it to George Cockayne for forty-four hundred dollars. Mr. Cockayne was a grocer, at that time located on Phillips Street, but the Directory indicates that in 1813 he moved his business to the basement store in his Anderson Street house. After his death, in 1830, his widow managed the store for a time, but apparently sold out the business in 1834. Mrs. Cockayne died in 1855, and the old house came into the possession of her daughter, Mrs. Francis B. Winter, who lived in the charming vineclad cottage that stood diagonally opposite until less than twenty years ago.

For many years, in its early history, the Cockayne house was a high-grade sailors' boarding-place. That was in the days when Boston was the home port of many clipper ships, and when it was the practice of ship masters to keep the unmarried and otherwise homeless members of their crews together between voyages by providing good boarding-places, a number of which were located on the Hill. After selling his South Russell Street house, Joseph Ditson seems to have gone into the business of boarding seamen, and for a time was located in a rented house on South Russell Street, later on Myrtle, and later still on Broad Street, which was nearer the docks. Incidentally Ditson was clerk of the militia for a number of years. For some time before Mrs. Cockayne's death, the basement store in her house had been rented as a fish market, kept at first by Solomon Newcomb, but after 1852 by Gilman D. Jackson. Mr. Jackson remained there until 1868, when he moved the store to 64 Anderson Street, where his sons still continue the business, now grown to something far different from the little neighborhood market that it was in its earlier years. The Cockayne house is another fine example of the good taste and craftsmanship of its day, and it has happily escaped the desecrating hand of the modernizer, its wainscoting, window-shutters, tooled fire-frames, and huge English door locks remaining exactly as of yore.

Just one hundred years ago, in 1824, the school-

house on the corner of Pinckney and Anderson
Streets was built to house the English High School.
Although this school was authorized by vote of the
town in 1820, and classes had been organized since
1821, this was the first building devoted exclusively
to its uses. It may be interesting, in passing, to
note the subjects that in those days were taught
to 'lads intending to become merchants or mechanics.' The courses of the first year included 'in-
tellectual' and written arithmetic, geography and
'the use of the globes,' grammar, general history,
United States history, single-entry bookkeeping,
'elements of some of the arts and sciences,' composition and declamation. During the second and
third years the students were given geometry,
algebra, trigonometry, double-entry bookkeeping,
'various branches of natural philosophy,' natural
history, chemistry, moral philosophy, natural
theology, rhetoric, evidences of Christianity, 'in-
tellectual philosophy,' political economy, logic, and
French. The land for the school-house was bought
in 1823 in two lots, Jesse Shaw selling the Anderson
Street frontage twenty-seven feet wide on Pinckney
Street, and the Mount Vernon Proprietors the
adjoining fifty-three feet on Pinckney Street.
Many years later, the Anderson Street side was
widened by purchasing a portion of the garden
belonging to the house next north.

This land had remained vacant all those years,

perhaps because of the presence directly across Pinckney Street of the stable attached to the Mount Vernon Street house built by Harrison Gray Otis, or, perhaps, because some entertained doubts as to the real estate titles founded upon that portion of the Copley purchase frequently referred to in these chapters as the subject of protracted litigation. This lot was not a part of the disputed Phillips pasture, to be sure, its nearest boundary to the Anderson Street corner being opposite Louisburg Square, so that any possible nervousness as to the title of the corner lot was unfounded in fact. The corner lot, twenty-seven feet wide on Pinckney Street, was bought by Hammond, Swett, and Farley from the Mount Vernon Proprietors as a part of a larger purchase, including 57 to 65 Pinckney Street. The portion east of Anderson they sold to John Pratt and others, who built the houses there before 1808. The lot under the school corner changed hands several times down to 1810, at prices close to one dollar a square foot, but no one built upon it. For thirteen years just prior to its purchase by the city, this lot was held in an unsettled estate. In 1823, it was transferred twice for about thirty-five cents a foot, and in the same year was sold to the city for just under sixty cents a foot.

In another chapter it was stated that, in 1805, Charles Bulfinch, the architect, bought the land now represented by 87 and 89 Mount Vernon Street and 68 to 78 Pinckney Street. The next year he began the erection of two houses on the Mount Vernon Street sites, but sold them before completion. This left the Pinckney Street frontage in his hands for a time. After the passage of sundry mesne conveyances, the westerly portion of this land came into the possession of Israel Thorndike and William J. Loring, who sold it, in 1829, to David Greenough. The easterly portion had been divided into lots owned by Howard Bowker, Joel Gustine, and the Honorable Francis Dana. Bowker sold, in 1824, for about half what he paid for this portion eighteen years before. In 1831, there was a wooden dwelling on this lot, according to the inventory of the estate of George Shepherd, who then owned an undivided half-interest. Greenough cut up the westerly portion into three front lots and one in the rear. The latter is the site of 74½ and the back yards of 76 and 78.

In 1829, Hollis Chapin bought a front lot, and the entire rear lot, and on October 5th of that year, entered into a contract (L. 341, f. 85) with Phineas Weeks and Amos Perrin for the building of the house, now Number 74, from plans by John Kutts, an architect with office at 31 Court Street. The house was to be completed within nine months, the contractors to furnish all materials, and the stipulated compensation was twenty-nine hundred dollars plus the rear lot of 1856 square feet, the latter being subject to a mortgage of four hundred dollars. This contract was discharged May 11, 1830. The specifications included sidewalk and edgestones, marble chimney pieces in the parlors to be worth from ninety to one hundred dollars a pair, three good coats of lead and oil paint on the interior finish, and the exterior brick walls to be weather-proofed with oil. Wall-papers where used were to cost various prices up to one dollar a roll. A cistern, pump, and twelve-gallon copper boiler were also included. In 1830, this house was assessed to David Chapin as unfinished. Soon after the completion of the house, Chapin sold to Ebenezer T. Pope, handcartman, for four thousand dollars, and he transferred it shortly after to Charles McIntire, broker, for a like sum. McIntire probably bought it on speculation, but real estate in that vicinity was in the doldrums just then, and after two years he sold to George Gregerson, master mariner, and took a loss of five hundred dollars. Gregerson lived there for some years, but the property eventually came into the possession of Noah Bodge whose heirs are the owners to-day.

The lot in the rear, given by Chapin in part payment for his house, became divided, Weeks and Perrin holding the westerly half, now the back yards of 76 and 78, and another firm of masons, Pierce and Parker, holding the east half, now the

THE MISLOCATED HOUSE, 33 REVERE STREET

ECCENTRIC WALL OF MR. OTIS'S STABLE

site of 74½. The latter lot was sold to Joshua and
Benjamin Turner, housewrights, in January, 1831,
for nine hundred and thirty-three dollars and in
October, 1833, Joshua bought out Benjamin for
two hundred and fifty dollars. The following year
a house is found on this lot assessed to Joshua
and occupied by Thomas W. Haskins, hardware
dealer. Such appears to have been the genesis of
what is known in the neighborhood as 'the hidden
house,' a thoroughly Old World location, approached from Pinckney Street through an iron-
gated arched passage, and walled around by the
houses of two streets, but yet with room sufficient
for a bit of garden along its southern wall.

In January, 1834, Greenough sold the lots under
76 and 78 to Samuel H. Mitchell and Loring
Dunbar, housewrights, and when the assessors
made their rounds that spring they recorded that
these two houses were 'mostly finished — erecting.'
Before another year, Joshua Bennett, of Billerica,
became the owner of 78 and not long after of 76,
and, in 1843, Turner sold to him the 'hidden house'
as well. These properties are still in that family.

One of the most curious eccentricities is found in
the rear brick wall of Mr. Otis's stable behind his
Beacon Street house. An alley opening on the east
side of Spruce Street leads to the stable, and any
one interested in freaks or in the art of brick-
masonry will find here something quite out of the

usual. Either through ignorance of his craft, or owing to some temporary aberration, perchance due to an unusually potent morning dram, the mason laid up the first thirty courses or so parallel to the grade of the alley, which pitches perceptibly to Spruce Street. At that point some one must have discovered what was happening, but instead of tearing down the wall and beginning anew, shims were inserted along the top of the sloping wall to true it up, and the job proceeded in horizontal courses thence to the eaves.

XVIII

OF SHADE-TREES AND GARDENS

THEY must have been tree-lovers, those men who developed the southwest slope of Beacon Hill for residential use a century and a quarter ago. Not only did they name a majority of the streets that they laid out after native trees, but they also planted many trees along those streets and on their private grounds. Most of the original street names have persisted — Chestnut, Walnut, Spruce, Acorn, Cedar, and Willow (the latter originally known as Maple) — and here and there a tree remains which, from its size, suggests the possibility that it was planted when those streets were relatively new. It has already been stated that Olive, the former name of Mount Vernon Street, was not original with the syndicate, being found in deeds as far back as 1735. Why it was so named no one seems to know, but it would appear more reasonable to presume that it was in honor of some woman, a relative, perhaps, of an abutting landowner, than for a tree of a species that never grew in these parts. It is unlikely that any of the original pasture trees survived the radical grading operations incident to the laying-out of the streets and lots. If that is so, then none of the larger trees now standing, outside of the Common, are more than one hundred and twenty-five years old. Taking into consideration the dates on which the various streets were cut through and built upon, and the changes that have taken place since then, it is unwarrantable to speak with great confidence as to the age of any of the existing trees, with the possible exception of some on the Common.

The streets first to be built upon after the Mount Vernon Proprietors began operations were: Beacon, Walnut, Chestnut (mainly from Walnut to Spruce), Mount Vernon (from Joy to just above Louisburg Square), Pinckney (from Joy to Anderson), and Charles Street. Myrtle, another botanically named street, was built up at about the same time, but under that other syndicate composed of Messrs. Hammond, Swett, and Farley. So far as can be learned, no trees were ever planted within the highway limits on Beacon, Walnut, Pinckney, Spruce, Willow, and Myrtle Streets. In most cases these were doubtless deemed too narrow to afford planting space. On Beacon and Pinckney Streets some of the earlier houses were detached and surrounded by garden space in which fruit and shade-trees were set out. A few of those side yards are still unbuilt upon, and there is a possibility that some of the original trees remain in those situations.

OF SHADE-TREES AND GARDENS

Upper Chestnut Street was set on both sides with lindens, but it is suspected that this was not done much if any before 1830, at which time the houses below Willow Street were built. The older trees now standing are apparently of about the same age throughout the length of the street. Fifty years ago there were many well-grown lindens on the easterly side of Charles Street between Pinckney and Cambridge Streets, and at the same period there were a number of large elms on Mount Vernon Street between Walnut and Willow Streets. Some of those elms still stand, but, looking at them to-day and trying to visualize them as they appeared to boyish eyes fifty years ago, it seems as if they, and the Chestnut Street lindens as well, had stood stock-still through all those years. And the same is true of the line of horse-chestnuts in front of 85 Mount Vernon Street, all but one of which have now gone.

But the finest trees on the Hill are those on private land, many of which are in back yards and never seen except by owners of adjacent houses, and by the men who deliver bundles and provisions at the rear doors. And few would suspect that many of these back yards are anything but deserts of brick paving. In the early days of the Hill, it was the pleasant custom to lay out these yards as gardens, and not a few still persist, some well-kept and cultivated, with paved paths between flowering beds, while all that remains of others are occasional pear trees, or more frequently great lilac thickets ten feet or more high.

Several remarkably fine trees of various species are found in some of these yards to-day, and it is a cause for wonder that, even where they have received no special care, they are, in most instances, in much thriftier condition than any of the trees on the near-by Common or streets. The elms, in most cases, show no sign of having suffered by leopard moth attacks, the cause of much mutilation elsewhere. Cooped up in a narrow north-facing yard in the rear of Beacon Street, just east of Charles Street, and all but surrounded by four-story houses, there is a monstrous horse-chestnut of graceful form and remarkable thriftiness. In view of the fact that the original house on this lot, together with several of its neighbors, was burned in that terrific fire of 1824, it is assumed that this tree was planted sometime after that event, perhaps by William Minot, the then owner. Another horse-chestnut of almost equal size stands in the rear of the Women's City Club, 40 Beacon Street, but it is not as full-crowned and symmetrical as the one farther down the street. That house, it has been seen, was built in 1818 on the site of one of Copley's houses, and perhaps the tree was planted soon after.

The next largest tree is a spreading American

THE GREAT HORSE–CHESTNUT IN THE BACK YARD OF
61 BEACON STREET

Probably planted about 1824

elm in the garden of the Appalachian Mountain Club at 5 Joy Street. There are two elms here marking the back corners of the lot. Both are large trees, but the one in the northwest angle has evidently profited by a more abundant feeding area and is the greater in girth and spread. An ancient horse-chestnut in the same enclosure has suffered the loss of a part of its head and in other ways shows signs of decrepit venerability. This lot was part of the garden of Thomas Perkins from 1805 until 1834, when the present house was built. A number of men, wise in matters arboreal, have registered guesses as to the age of these trees, which vary all the way from ninety to one hundred and twenty years.

On the front lawn of 82 Mount Vernon Street there stands a most perfect specimen of a tulip poplar. This tree has been trimmed of its lower branches to a considerable height so that its clean, straight shaft rises to the level of the third-story windows, and supports a symmetrical, wide-branching head. In an adjacent yard are several honey-locusts of large size and another of this species is found in a lawn at the corner of Joy Street and Mount Vernon Place. No one seems to know the ages of these trees. The Joy Street house dates from 1824 and those on Mount Vernon Street from 1834.

The linden is a species that seems to do exceptionally well in the gravelly soil of the Hill, and those in narrow back yards are head and shoulders above the best now standing on the streets. In the rear of 45 Beacon Street, on what was a part of the side garden of the Harrison Gray Otis house until 1831, there is a group of lindens of impressive size and taller than the close surrounding houses. Another tall and equally handsome specimen stands in the rear of 49 Pinckney Street, its topmost branches waving luxuriantly many feet above the neighboring roof-tops. Two other good-sized lindens stand in the lawn of 85 Mount Vernon Street, where Mr. Otis lived before moving to Beacon Street.

White ash is another tree that, until within recent years, has been abundant and thrifty in many of the narrowest alleyways. The largest specimen, a widely branching tree of large girth, towers above the playground opposite the Bowdoin School on Myrtle Street. Of late the ashes have begun to fail, showing considerable dead wood in their tops, perhaps as a result of leopard moth infestation, or possibly because of San José scale, which often attacks this tree. Maples are few and far between on the Hill. The best specimen, a medium-sized tree, is one of the Norway variety on the lawn of 83 Mount Vernon Street.

The commonest tree found on the Hill, and especially in the yards on the northerly slope, is the ailanthus, or tree of heaven. No one, not even Professor Charles S. Sargent, of the Arboretum, knows when this Chinese tree was introduced into Boston. The Arboretum is authority for the information that it was first planted in America in 1784 by William Hamilton, whose gardens, near Philadelphia, were famous. In 1804, it was first brought into New England at Portsmouth, Rhode Island, and it is not impossible that specimens may have been set out in some of the Hill gardens about that time. Possibly it was not brought here until later, when, in 1820, there was a widespread demand for ailanthus in many Eastern cities, its graceful foliage, rapid growth, and general hardiness making it a great favorite. Unfortunately no discrimination was made between male and female trees, and complaints arose at the offensive odor of the blossoms, and that cistern water from the roofs was made unfit for use by the pollen that sometimes blew in clouds. A ruthless war was waged against the ailanthus as a result, and not until after most of the trees had fallen under the axe was it discovered that the flowers of the female tree are scentless, and that the male tree alone is responsible for the odor objected to by many.

Happily the ailanthus was by no means exterminated, so far as Beacon Hill was concerned. The largest specimen known in this section stood until January, 1924, in the front yard of 5 Joy Street, a tree as tall as the house and of very erect and handsome habit. During a storm it snapped off close to the ground where decay, due to some injury, had reduced its fiber to a mere shell. Harris A. Reynolds, Secretary of the Massachusetts Forestry Association, examined the tree at that time and estimated its age at between fifty-six and sixty years. The growth rings showed that it attained a diameter of six inches within the first ten years of its life, and that up to its fortieth year it made steady progress. Then suddenly its growth all but ceased, and for the last twenty years the rings were so close as to be read with difficulty even under a lens. Two of the best remaining specimens are growing within the narrow limits of side yards on upper Pinckney Street, both standing close to the street line, with their branches extending well out over the roadway. Both are distinctly ornaments to that narrow street.

Although there are systematic records dating back to 1844 relative to the management of Louisburg Square, nothing can be found to show when the older trees were planted. The grassed oval was widened in 1844, and it is not improbable that the trees were planted at that time or soon after. The engraving showing the Square as it appeared in the early fifties pictures the trees as perhaps eight or ten inches in diameter. Several of the older trees have died in recent years, but those veterans

AN ANCIENT LINDEN TREE IN A PINCKNEY
STREET BACK YARD

Probably planted before 1810

A CORNER OF ONE OF THE BACK-YARD GARDENS

10 Walnut Street, formerly the home of

Robert C. Winthrop

that remain appear to be not more than eighty years old.

Just inside the Common, along the Beacon Street Mall between Park and Joy Streets, there stand eight huge English elms. These are probably the oldest trees on any part of the Hill to-day, and it is believed that they were planted by order of John Hancock in the fall of 1780. The largest of the eight, the one just inside the fence opposite 33 Beacon Street, the Park Department building, was the subject of an interesting monograph, 'The Life of Campestris Ulm, the Oldest Inhabitant of Boston Common,' by Joseph Henry Curtis, 1910. It there appears, in a quotation from the Selectmen's records, that on October 26, 1780, His Excellency, John Hancock, petitioned 'for liberty to break ground near his seat for the pulling up of old trees and putting down others in their room,' and that 'liberty was accordingly granted' and a committee named to 'view the bank near his home.' It is not improbable that all were planted at that time.

Just across the mall from the big tree, and at the junction of the broad path leading to Winter Street, is the gingko tree that was moved to this location from the Gardiner Greene place in Pemberton Square in 1834.

Only a few yards from the gingko, on the eastern side of the path to West Street, are two large lindens with a young tree between, and the second of these larger trees the Park Department has reason to believe is not far from a century old. Using that tree as a yardstick with which to measure the largest lindens already referred to as standing in the yards on Beacon, Mount Vernon, and Pinckney Streets, it is easy to believe that most of these have seen one hundred years or more.

XIX

EARLY ARCHITECTS AND BUILDERS

THROUGHOUT these pages there have been frequent references to the men who designed or built some of the early houses on the Hill. Information as to the architects and craftsmen of that day is scanty and scattered, and the facts presented here, admittedly fragmentary, have been gathered from many sources. Inquiries made of members of the architectural profession well posted in the known history of that period only served to confirm the belief that there was little dependable material available for use in this chapter. After much searching through various architectural works, biographies, and sundry public documents and records, it has been possible to gather enough facts for a few sketchy paragraphs.

It has been the not uncommon custom to assume that Charles Bulfinch was responsible for the design of any building of architectural merit built in Boston between 1790 and 1818. After the latter date, and until 1830, Bulfinch lived in Washington as the architect of the Capitol, and from the time of his return to Boston until his death in 1844, he does not appear to have practiced his profession to any appreciable extent. Beyond doubt Bulfinch

273

was, for many years, the best-known member of his profession in this section, for his practice was large and included many of the important public buildings of Boston, and not a few of the handsomer residences of the period were doubtless of his designing. He was not, however, the only man in practice here, though for some time, or until 1806, he seems to have been the only one to call himself an architect.

One of Bulfinch's early contemporaries, Asher Benjamin, recorded in 1823 [1] that 'The time has been, within my own recollection, when New England did not contain a single professed architect. The first individual who laid claim to that character was Charles Bulfinch, Esq., of this city; to whose classical taste we are indebted for many fine buildings.' In this connection Benjamin added that 'The construction of the Franklin Street houses, of which that gentleman was the Architect, gave the first impulse to good taste; and Architecture, in this part of the country, has advanced with accelerated progress ever since.' The Franklin Street houses referred to constituted the block of residences on what was originally known as 'Franklin Place,' between Hawley and Devonshire Streets, and called the 'Tontine Crescent.' Bulfinch not only designed these buildings, but was a

[1] Introduction, *Practice of Architecture*, by Asher Benjamin. Boston, 1823.

54 AND 55 BEACON STREET
Perhaps by Asher Benjamin, 1807
Prescott, the historian, lived in the upper house

partner in the development. Hard times came on shortly after their completion, 1793–96, and the partners found themselves seriously embarrassed. Indeed, Bulfinch's resources were entirely exhausted, his own house in Bowdoin Street being sold over his head. William Scollay was also interested in the Crescent buildings, and both he and Bulfinch, as elsewhere previously noted, were at that time associated with Mason and Otis in the Mount Vernon Proprietors' undertaking. Both were obliged to withdraw from that venture, Benjamin Joy and Mrs. Swan being the purchasers of their shares.

Prior to Bulfinch the native housewrights had for the most part shown the good sense to follow the dictates of various books on domestic architecture written by English practitioners of high standing. The works of R. and S. Adam and of William and James Pain seem to have circulated widely here from 1773 to 1822 or thereabouts.[1] In his scholarly work (1922), 'Domestic Architecture of the American Colonies and the Early Republic,' Fiske Kimball states that 'A native

---

[1] *The City and Country Builder's and Workman's Treasury of Designs,* illustrated with upward of 400 designs from copper plates, by B. L., London, 1750 (a copy formerly owned by Benjamin, with his autograph, reprinted by Boston Architectural Club, 1922). *Works in Architecture,* R. and S. Adam, London, 1773. *The Practical Builder,* 1792, and *The Practical House Carpenter,* 1796, by W. and J. Pain (some reprinted in Boston). *Town and Country Builder's Assistant,* by J. Norman, Boston.

version of the Adam forms was embodied by a Massachusetts builder, Asher Benjamin, in his first two works.' Benjamin was a Boston housewright and contractor and several good houses still stand to his credit on Beacon Hill.

In his chapter on 'Architecture in Boston' in the 'Memorial History,' Charles A. Cummings wrote that 'Asher Benjamin is less remembered for his buildings than for his books.' [1] Continuing, he stated that 'These were what their titles implied — practical guides to the builder who undertook the duties of both carpenter and architect; and from the faithful study of them grew the classic house-fronts and interior details of a generation to which systematic architectural education was as yet unknown.' In three houses on Bowdoin Street, opposite Derne, built by Benjamin in 1825, he carried out some of his classical ideals in the capitals of the entrance porticoes and in the carved brownstone window caps. Number 9 West Cedar Street is another of his houses, built in 1833, and the church at the corner of Mount Vernon and Charles Streets, built in 1807, is generally regarded as of his designing.

During the first eighteen years of the last century, or until Bulfinch accepted the commission at

[1] *The Country Builder's Assistant*, 1796; *American Builder's Companion*, 1806; *Rudiments of Architecture*; *The Builder's Guide*; *Architect; or Practical House Carpenter*, 1840.

Washington, there were several men in Boston who furnished architectural plans. For the most part these were artisans who had, presumably, taken a reading course in architectural design with the aid of some of the books already mentioned. It is generally believed, though not perhaps susceptible of positive documentary proof, that Bulfinch planned a number of the best of the early houses on the Hill, among them the Mason and Thomas Perkins houses on Mount Vernon Street, both long since demolished; Numbers 6 and 8, 13, 15, and 17 Chestnut Street, also 29A, the latter probably the first house built in that section; the three Otis houses, on Cambridge, Mount Vernon, and Beacon Streets, all still standing; also 49 to 57 Mount Vernon Street, all except 55 now much altered in appearance; doubtless 87 Mount Vernon, which is quite unchanged; and 39 and 40 Beacon Street. A fourth story was added to the last two, and central windows were cut in the bay of Number 39, about 1887. Otherwise those houses are little changed. A number of other distinctly good, though less distinguished early houses on the Hill were probably designed by their builders, a number of speculative housewrights. From 1796 until 1810, Jeremiah Gardner was the most active of this latter group, and many of his houses on Pinckney, Joy, Mount Vernon, Chestnut, and Beacon Streets remain but little altered.

Jesse Shaw, who had been a journeyman in Gardner's employ, set up for himself in 1810, and during his long and active life he built a number of the houses on and around the Hill; several on Louisburg Square and on Mount Vernon and Pinckney Streets near the Square were among the latest of his construction. Ephraim Marsh, who is first found in the Directory of 1798, built Numbers 1, 3, and 5 Chestnut Street (the first two still standing), and several on Mount Vernon Street that have been superseded. Excepting the church at the corner of Mount Vernon and Charles Streets (1807), no building of earlier date than 1825 has been positively traced to Benjamin, though the title records lead one to suspect that he built some of the houses on Charles and Beacon Streets that were destroyed by the fire of 1824. Joseph Lincoln and Hezekiah Stoddard were in partnership as housewrights for twenty years or more. In 1811, they built Number 62 Chestnut Street, and in 1817 Number 64. These houses were burned in 1824, but were immediately rebuilt; in 1827 and 1828, Numbers 66 and 68 were also erected. In 1830 they bought a piece of Jonathan Mason's garden, fronting on Pinckney Street, and built the houses now numbered 12 and 14. Stoddard himself, and after him his son-in-law, Seth Thomas, lived for many years at 64 Chestnut Street, and 12 Pinckney has continued to the present time to be the residence of the Lincoln family.

EARLY ARCHITECTS AND BUILDERS

There were also professed architects in Boston during the first two decades of the nineteenth century. In 1806, Peter Banner is found in the Directory calling himself 'architect, 29 Orange Street.' Banner was an Englishman. In 1809 he built Park Street Church and in 1825 he was supervising architect of Bunker Hill Monument. It may be that he designed some of the residences on the Hill during that period, but no proof of this has been found. Solomon Willard entered the field in 1810 as a carver in wood and stone, but seems to have devoted himself to the study of architecture meantime, for in 1819 he was associated with Alexander Parris in the design of Saint Paul's Church. The capitals on the Park Street spire are said to have been his work. Parris first appears in the Directory in 1816 and as an architect. Saint Paul's Church was one of his earliest public works, but a year earlier he began the residence of David Sears, now the Somerset Club, on Beacon Street. Willard was also associated in this house, at least to the extent of carving the ornamental panels of the façade. In 1824, Parris designed the house of George Williams Lyman at the corner of Mount Vernon and Joy Streets. Both the Sears and the Lyman houses remain, though the former has been doubled in size and otherwise modified by two or three subsequent changes. Parris was also the architect of the Marine Hospital at

Chelsea, the Watertown Arsenal, and the Quincy Market.

Banner's name continued in the Directory through 1828, Willard's through 1837, while Parris is found through 1850, and for a part of this time he was listed as an engineer as well as architect. In the twenties four new names appear in the Directory as architects, Cornelius Coolidge in 1823, Isaiah Rogers in 1827, John Kutts and Edward Shaw in 1828. Through recorded building contracts the names of all except Rogers are connected with houses on the Hill. His nearest known connection with the architecture of that section was in the plan for the Tremont House in 1829, but, as he continued in practice through 1847, it is not impossible that he may have had a hand in some of the residences. The only house on the Hill that the writer has been able to trace definitely to Kutts is 76 Pinckney Street, built in 1828 (L. 341, f. 85), but as he continues in the Directory through 1838 it is not impossible that other houses there may be to his credit.

The first mention of Edward Shaw in the Directory is in 1823, when he was listed as a housewright, and as such he continued to be rated until 1828, when he is found with an office in State Street as an architect. Although he continued in practice through 1855 at various addresses, there is but one house on the Hill that the writer feels reasonably certain was from his designs. In 1837, Adam Wallace Thaxter, Jr., the mathematical instrument maker, built 59 Mount Vernon Street, the house which was later the home of T. B. Aldrich. In the recorded building contract it is stated that the plans were by 'Mr. Shaw' (L. 417, f. 95). Since Jesse Shaw, housewright, was active in building a number of houses in and near Louisburg Square at that time, it might be assumed that he was the Mr. Shaw referred to except for the fact that Jesse Shaw was not the contractor for Thaxter, and for the further fact that this house is quite different in design from any attributed to him. Its details indicate the hand of an artist rather than that of a skilled artisan. Edward Shaw was also the author of a book entitled 'Civil Architecture' that ran through at least four editions, the last printed in 1836.

Cornelius Coolidge, who permitted his name to appear for but one year in the Directory as an architect, was the probable designer of somewhere in the vicinity of fifty houses between the State House and Charles Street, principally on the John Hancock property and on Chestnut, West Cedar, and Acorn Streets. In 1823, he was listed in the Directory as an architect with an office at 5 State Street, but thereafter he appeared as a building contractor, and occasionally the words 'real estate broker' or 'real estate agent' were added. It has elsewhere been stated that he was closely associated with John Hubbard in the development of the Hancock property and other Hill lots, and in many instances it is obvious that Coolidge built on his own account as his contracts with various house-wrights and other mechanics bear testimony.

Before his entering the building field, Coolidge's name is found in the Directory from 1803 through 1822 as a merchant on Long Wharf. The record of his death in the city archives, in 1843, gives his age as sixty-five, which would make 1778 the date of his birth. His name is not found in the scanty Boston birth records of that period. He was therefore twenty-five years old when he began as a merchant, and forty-five when he appeared on State Street as an architect. In a pamphlet written by Coolidge in connection with an unfortunate speculation in lands on Boston Neck, bought of the city in 1825, and printed as a part of an official report by a committee of the Common Council in 1833, he implied that he had been the victim of persecution by members of the City Government who were envious of his prosperity. In this connection he stated that 'Without patrimony or public office the subscriber has hitherto relied upon his own exertion and industry for his support,' which is an indication that he was a self-made man. In the portion of the document written by the committee it was stated that Coolidge had been 'reduced from affluence to insolvency' as a result of the financial crisis of 1829, which year, the report states, 'is memorable for the distress brought upon the manufacturing and other great interests of the city and Commonwealth, and it is within the knowledge of the Council that many of our wealthiest families and citizens were ruined.'

While he was still in mercantile business, in 1811, Coolidge bought land on Allston Street, opposite the head of Bulfinch, and built twin houses of some architectural pretension which still remain. This may have been his maiden effort in the new field. His enterprises with Hubbard and independently on the Hill began in 1824 and ended, for the most part, in 1829. Immediately following that Common Council report of 1833, which seems to have led to a settlement of the city's claim against Coolidge for those Neck lands, he managed to get on his feet again in a measure. It was then that he built the block of houses now numbered 1 to 4 Joy Street, and furnished the plans for 36 Beacon Street. In 1838, he bought 57 Mount Vernon Street and made extensive alterations in this old Bulfinch house, in the course of which, it will be recalled, the original front door was swallowed up in the addition. According to the Directory of 1840, he was living in that house, but the next year he was listed at 64 Belknap (Joy) Street, the site of which is now in the school yard close to Cambridge Street. This was far from being a fashionable neighborhood even in that day, and the inference is that Coolidge had again lost his hold, a conclusion that seems to be borne out by the fact that his name does not appear in the records of the Probate Court where it certainly would have been found had he left any property. His wife was a daughter of Moses Grant, Sr., the fashionable upholsterer from about 1789 to 1816, and who lived at 74 Mount Vernon Street in a house which he built in 1810. Coolidge was buried in his own lot in the Granary Burying Ground.

In 1834, another English architect, Richard Upjohn, came to Boston and was in practice here for a number of years. It was he who designed the Gothic fence around the Common, and in 1847 he built the brownstone houses on Mount Vernon Street for John E. and Nathaniel Thayer, now the Theological School. He was also noted as the architect of Trinity Church, New York. Two other brownstone houses, 40 and 42 Mount Vernon Street, at the corner of Walnut, were built by Alfred Hemenway in 1850 from plans by George M. Dexter. Until 1847 Dexter was listed in the Directory as a merchant, but after that date he appears as an architect, though without any change in business address, 11½ Tremont Row.

The architecture of the older houses on the Hill might be termed thoroughbred. Even in the most costly houses built during the first thirty

years of the last century there is nothing preten-
tious, while the less costly ones are anything but
mean, and carry a dignity and charm that is
traceable to their admirable proportions and to
the tasteful interior and exterior details. And
this is as true of many of the houses designed by
artisans as it is of those credited to the professed
architects. There is a strong individuality about
many of the houses, and there are likewise architectural mannerisms that, in not a few instances,
betray the period of the structure to the practiced
eye, and in some cases even serve to identify the
designer with reasonable certainty.

With a few exceptions brick houses built before
1810 on all sides of the Hill, and some of the finer
ones of later date, were laid up in Flemish bond, at
least in the front walls. Side walls, even when
exposed, and sometimes back walls, of such houses
were usually laid up with from five to twelve
courses of stretchers (the long way of the brick)
with one course of headers (the end way of the
brick). The Ditson house, at 43 South Russell
Street (1797 or 1798), was one of the exceptions,
all walls being laid seven and one. In 29A Chestnut
Street, not unlikely by Bulfinch (1799 or 1800),
the exposed flat walls are Flemish, but the wide
bow on the street side is twelve and one, which
possibly is an indication that this feature was of
later date. It is quite probable that the house was

remodeled by Charles R. Codman who bought it in 1818. After 1810, most front walls were laid with invisible bonds, all brick being laid the long way on the exposed face for the full height of the house.

It is stated by Mr. Kimball in his 'Domestic Architecture' that the habit of painting brick houses, usually gray, was introduced by Bulfinch about 1793, his Franklin Place block being so treated. This was doubtless for water-proofing as the old porous brick absorbed much moisture, thus rendering the imperfectly warmed houses damp. In the Kirk Boot residence on Bowdoin Square it is said that the bricks were all dipped, before being laid, in a mixture containing molasses. In some instances insulating spaces nearly a foot wide were left between the inner faces of brick walls and the studding. It was not uncommon, Mr. Kimball states, to sheathe brick walls on the outside with close-jointed boarding instead of clapboards, a feature which he says was familiar in Bulfinch's work. The Callender house, 14 Walnut Street, is an example of this practice, though this house has never been attributed to Bulfinch.

Bulfinch is also credited by Mr. Kimball with having set the fashion of facing houses on their side yards where the lots were relatively narrow. Houses which he is believed to have designed on Mount Vernon Street, now 49, 55, and 57, were so built and 55 so remains. Others copied the idea, and

286

some of the houses on upper Pinckney Street, that no one ever suspected Bulfinch of designing, are so constructed. There were also instances of this kind even before Bulfinch went into practice, and the houses built by Bela Clap, 44 and 46 Temple Street, some two or three years before Bulfinch began his career, face on narrow side yards. Several early frame houses still remain, and an examination of those structures shows that those built after 1798 (and the Temple Street houses are believed to be the only ones of earlier date now standing) had either one of the long sides or both ends of brick. This was in conformity with a statute of 1798. This statute provided, furthermore, that 'no brick or stone wall shall be deemed sufficient . . . unless the same shall be at least twelve inches thick above the lower story.'

This same statute required that all roofs should thereafter be 'entirely covered with slate, tile, or some incombustible composition.' Shingled roofs had been common until that time, and it is known that in some cases sheds and other outbuildings in yards, built subsequent to that enactment, were shingled, and that shingled house roofs were re-shingled after that date, perhaps unlawfully in all cases. At least one shingled house roof remains on the Hill at the present time. That house antedates the statute by perhaps ten years, and it is inconceivable that the original roof covering could have lasted through nearly one hundred and forty years.

Flat roofs were not uncommon before 1810. The fact that the Ditson house on South Russell Street is flat-roofed to-day is no proof, of course, that it was so built. The houses now numbered 58 Anderson and 25 and 27 Pinckney Street, built before 1810, are also flat-roofed and apparently always were so. What material was used for roofing these houses in those days has not been discovered, though considerable inquiry has been made into the history of the roofing trade in an effort to determine this fact. It is well known that in expensive houses sheet lead was used for flat roofs, both in this country and in England, at a very early date. Copper was also used, but, like lead, this was costly. Mr. Kimball is authority for the information that tin was a good deal employed in the early days of the Republic, and that Thomas Jefferson was an advocate of that material. The so-called felt or composition roofing appears to have originated in Boston, but not until about the middle of the last century. None of the houses mentioned were expensive ones — indeed they were economically built — and it is therefore unlikely that either lead or copper was used upon their roofs. The words of the statute above quoted as to an 'incombustible composition' leads one to assume that there may have been some form of

NEWEL-POST AND MANTEL-DETAIL OF BELA CLAP HOUSE

roof covering at that period other than stone or metal.

Window lintels, even more than doors or doorways, are suggestive of periods and of designers. The keystone, both double and single, ornamented and plain, was typical of Bulfinch, as was the band course of stone or raised brick, between the first and second stories, and the recessed arches surrounding first-floor windows. Instances of these features are seen in 55 Mount Vernon Street and in 13 to 17 Chestnut Street. Lintels carved in Greek key center patterns (later with bow knots) with rosette ends, the latter sometimes turned either up or down, came into vogue about 1818, one of the earliest examples being in 39 and 40 Beacon Street, presumably Bulfinch houses. This style continued until the late thirties, though in less elaborate forms, as in the houses now numbered 1 to 4 Joy Street. Asher Benjamin laid down the dictum in one of his books that all such ornament should be cut in relief, since an inscribed line gave a sense of weakness. In the later examples, however, the patterns were, for the most part, cut into the stone, probably for the reason that this was a less expensive practice. Benjamin, nevertheless, seems to have lived up to his doctrine in his own practice, as is witnessed by the houses which he built at 92, 94, and 98 (*sic*) Bowdoin Street in 1825.

On some Hill streets, notably on Chestnut and

West Cedar, but also on Joy, Hancock, and Myrtle Streets, triple square-headed windows with narrow side-lights are locally characteristic features. Mr. Kimball states that Bulfinch introduced this form in the Joseph Barrell mansion at Charlestown. These windows do not figure in any of the houses most surely attributed to Bulfinch on the Hill, however. The houses on Joy, Hancock, and Myrtle Streets having such windows were probably designed by the housewrights who built them, all dating from about 1806. Those on Chestnut and West Cedar Streets, where these window forms are much better proportioned, are in houses presumably designed by Cornelius Coolidge in the twenties.

Long windows reaching to the floor, mainly on the second or parlor story, Mr. Kimball also credits to Bulfinch. They are found in several of the best houses generally accredited to him, such as the Otis houses on Mount Vernon and Beacon Streets. These windows were sometimes composed of three sets of guillotine sash, and sometimes of French casement sash.

Speaking of windows calls to mind that other well-known characteristic of some of the early houses, notably in Beacon Street, their much-cherished panes of purple glass. This embellishment is found only in windows dating between 1818 and 1824, and not by any means in all houses built or altered during that period even in the same neighborhood or block. Although much prized to-day by those whose houses are thus distinguished, the color was purely a matter of accident. The builders of those houses had no intention of adorning them with windows of tinted glass, and it is not suspected that the manufacturers had any thought of turning out other than an article of the usual high-grade standard. Sunlight and time, however, developed a change which is said to be due to a gradual chemical transformation of one of the elements (oxide of manganese) in the particular batch of glass used in certain houses. Eventually those windows assumed a delicate lilac hue, and lilac they have since remained to the joy and pride, rather than to the chagrin, of their owners. This glass was not peculiar to Boston, though, for Robert Shackleton in 'The Book of Boston' claims a similar distinction for certain old houses in Irving Place and Clinton Place, New York. There are but few remaining examples in Boston, the present proud possessors being 39, 40, 63, 64, and 70 Beacon Street, and 29A Chestnut Street.

THE END

INDEX

Acorn Street, 185, 186.
Adam, R. and S., work on architecture, 275.
Adams, Benjamin, 130.
Adams, Charles Francis, Minister to England during the Civil War, 211.
Adams, James H., member of Proprietors' Committee of Louisburg Square, 192.
Adams, Joseph K., shoemaker, 234, 235.
Ailanthus, the, 268–70.
Alcott, Amos Bronson, 201.
Aldrich, Thomas Bailey, 211, 281.
Allen, Freeman, 134, 139.
Allen, Reverend James, 10, 17, 213, 251.
Allen, James, grandson of Reverend James, 213, 251.
Allen (James) pasture, 9–12, 61–63, 119, 213, 251.
Amory, Mrs. James S., 137.
Amory, Thomas Coffin, his biographical sketch of William Blaxton quoted, 203.
Amory, William, 178.
Anderson Street, 213; corner Myrtle Street, 217, 255, 256; corner Revere Street, 251–54; No. 64, 256; corner Pinckney Street, 256–68; No. 58, 288.
Andrews, Elizabeth, wife of Joseph Joy (2), 121.
Appalachian Mountain Club, house of, No. 5 Joy Street, 112, 142; tree in garden of, 267.
Appleton, Charlotte, first wife of Thomas Perkins, Sr., 106.
Appleton, Nathan, manufacturer, 172, 176.
Appleton, Nathaniel, 106.
Appleton, Samuel, 126, 134, 138.

Appleton, Thomas, American Consul at Leghorn, 108.
Appleton, Thomas Gold, 129.
Apthorp, C. W., 20.
Apthorp, John Trecothick, president of the Boston Bank, 181.
Architects, 273–84.
Architecture, of older houses on the Hill, thoroughbred, 284, 285; brick houses, 285, 286; houses facing on the side yard, 286, 287; roofs, 287, 288; window lintels, 289; windows, 290; window glass, 290, 291.
Armstrong, Samuel T., Mayor of Boston and Lieutenant-Governor of Massachusetts, 130, 133, 139.
Austin, Benjamin, 219, 220.
Austin, Jonathan, 219, 220.
Austin, Samuel, 178.

Babcock, Tristram, mariner, 225, 227, 229.
Back Bay, the, 47.
Baldwin, William H., president of the Boston Young Men's Christian Union, 103.
Baldwin, Mrs. William H., 103.
Ballou, Maturin M., 235.
Bangs, Benjamin, 207, 209.
Banner, Peter, architect, 279, 280.
Bannister, Thomas, 23, 26, 51.
'Bannister's Gardens,' 26.
Bardwell, Josiah, public spirit of, 140, 141.
Barge, Henry, fisherman, 244, 246.
Barrell, Hannah, wife of Benjamin Joy, 60, 122.
Barrell, Joseph, business man, 60, 122.
Barrett, James, 219.
Barrett, Mrs. James, 219.
Bartol, Elizabeth, 169.

293

INDEX

connection with Louisburg Square, 203, 204.

Bodge, Noah, 260.

Book of Possessions, 4.

Borland, John, 134, 139.

Boston, Massachusetts, real estate maps of, 4; early description of, 6.

Boston Park Department, headquarters of, 152.

Boston University Law School, 14.

Boston University School of Theology, 23, 159, 162, 166, 284.

Bosworth, Benjamin, 186.

Bosworth, Hiram, 186.

Bosworth, Zaccheus, 11, 20, 21, 147.

Bosworth (Zaccheus) pasture, 11, 20, 21, 61, 62.

Bowditch, Dr. Nathaniel, 1.

Bowditch, Nathaniel Ingersoll, 'Gleaner' articles on real estate titles on Beacon Hill, 1–4; references to his 'Gleaner' articles, 8–25, 27–31, 52, 58, 66, 80, 117–19, 125, 135, 136, 147, 215, 251, 252; witnesses Beacon Hill fire, 175; his spelling of Louisburg, 204.

Bowditch, William I., 191.

Bowdoin, pronunciation of the name, 168.

Bowdoin, James (1), father of Governor Bowdoin, 15.

Bowdoin, Governor James (2), 13, 15, 19, 49, 237.

Bowdoin house, on the site of the Bellevue and the Unitarian Society, 19, 20.

Bowdoin Square, Kirk Boot residence, 286.

Bowdoin Street, formerly called Middlecott Street, 13, 215; laid out, 20, 215; houses on, built by Benjamin, 276, 289.

Bowers, John, 18.

Bowker, Howard, 259.

Bowker, Theodore M., 183.

Bradlee, James Bowdoin, 155.

Bradstreet, William, 96.

Branch Street (formerly Kitchen Street), 170.

Breed, William, baker, 241.

Brewer, Gardner, 150.

Brewster, Charles W., maker of springs, 246, 247.

Brick houses, 285, 286.

Brick-masonry, freak in art of, 261, 262.

Brigham, Benajah, bricklayer, 248–50.

Bromfield, pronunciation of the name, 168.

Bromfield, Edward (1), residence of, 19, 49.

Bromfield, Edward (2), 106.

Bromfield, Mary, daughter of Edward Bromfield (2), wife of William Powell, 106.

Brooks, Peter C., 89.

Brown, Alice, 235.

Brown, Enoch, 61, 91, 220.

Brown (Enoch) pasture. See Bosworth pasture, Brown lands.

Brown, Josiah, housewright, 209.

Brown lands, purchased by Mount Vernon Proprietors, 61–63, 91, 119.

Bryant, John, 175, 176.

Bryant, John, Jr., agreement made by, with Proprietors' Committee of Louisburg Square, 192.

Building-costs, 207–12. See Prices.

Bulfinch, Charles, 13; designer of original monument on Beacon Hill, 30; member of syndicate, Mount Vernon Proprietors, 58–60, 275; deposition of, 58, 63, 69; his street scheme, 70–72; testimony as regards topography of Hill, 72–74; as regards the removal of Mount Vernon, 80; lot on Mount Vernon Street bought by, 87, 250, 259; divides Mount Vernon Street lot, 87, 88; sells property No. 87 Mount Vernon Street, 93; houses designed by, 171, 176; buildings for which he is responsible, 273–75, 277; introduced habit of painting brick houses, 286; keystone typical of, 289; his windows, 290.

Bulfinch, Dr. Thomas, 13.

295

INDEX

Bulfinch, Dr. William, 251, 252.

Bulfinch (Thomas) pasture, 13, 14, 215.

Bunker Hill Monument, architect of, 179, 279.

Burgess, Benjamin, agreement made by, with Proprietors' Committee of Louisburg Square, 192.

Burgess, B. F., member of standing committee of Louisburg Square Proprietors, 193, 194.

Burgess, Franklin, agreement made by, with Proprietors' Committee of Louisburg Square, 192.

Buttolph, Abigail, wife of Joseph Belknap, Jr., 214. See Belknap, Mrs. Joseph, Jr.

Buttolph, Mary, wife of Robert Guttridge, 214.

Buttolph, Nicholas, 214, 240.

Buttolph, Thomas, 12, 114, 214, 240.

Buttolph (Thomas) pasture, 12, 114, 214, 240.

Buttolph Street (Irving Street), 12, 214, 240.

Cabot, Samuel, 62, 66–69.

Cabot, Susan B., 155.

Cade, George, 220.

Cade, Peter, 220.

Calico printing establishment, Irving Street, 242.

Callender, John, lot on corner of Mount Vernon and Walnut Streets, 119, 120, 123, 136, 137, 160, 170; develops land on Mount Vernon Street, 128; house, No. 34, Mount Vernon Street, 128, 136.

Cambridge Street, house on, designed by Bulfinch, 277.

'Cape Cod Row,' Tremont Street, 138.

Carleton, Osgood, surveyor, 67, 187; his plan of the State House lot, 28.

Carlton, Sarah Sumner, 239.

Carnes, Edward, ropemaker, 248.

Carnes, Elizabeth (Fennecy), 242, 245, 248.

Carnes, Joseph, 61, 220.

Carnes, Thomas Jenner, rope manufacturer, 245, 248.

Cedar Lane, 83.

Cedar Lane Way, 83.

Chace, Caleb, 141.

Chaffee, George A., 102, 103.

Channing, Reverend William Ellery, residence of, 73, 74, 207, 212.

Chapin, David, 260.

Chapin, Hollis, 259.

Charles Street, laid out, 7, 31, 81, developed early as a residence street, 45; graded up, 170; as regards trees on, 264, 265; corner Mount Vernon Street, church designed by Benjamin, 276.

Chestnut Street, laid out, 79, 187; early nineteenth-century houses on, 84; No. 31, 108; Nos. 13, 15, and 17, 56 n., 168, 289; No. 54, 155; Nos. 29A–37, 160–65, 167, 277, 285, 291; Nos. 6 and 8, 166; Nos. 27 to 29, 166; Nos. 4 and 10, 166, 184; house on site of Theological School, 166; No. 2, 179; No. 42, 179; No. 44, 179; Nos. 62, 64, 66, and 68, 179, 180, 278; Nos. 23 and 25, 181; Nos. 22 and 24, 183; Nos. 12, 14, and 16, 183, 184; John Hubbard houses, 184; corner Walnut Street, 185; Nos. 1, 3, and 5, 185, 278; Nos. 50–60, 185; Nos. 70–76, 185; No. 61, 185; Nos. 39–45, and 55, 185; Nos. 47, 49, 51, and 53, 186; corner West Cedar Street, 186; as regards trees on, 264, 265; house on, designed by Bulfinch, 277; houses on, built by Marsh, 278; houses on, built by Lincoln and Stoddard, 278; No. 29A, 277, 285, 291; window lintels in Nos. 13 to 17, 289.

Chipman, John, mariner, 244, 246.

Claflin, Governor William, 211.

Clap, Bela, housewright, 237–39, 287.

Clap, Caleb, 238, 239.

Clapboard Street (Joy Street), 91, 115, 219, 220, 222.

INDEX

298

INDEX

Gibbs, Nathan B., agreement made by, with Proprietors' Committee of Louisburg Square, 192; member of first standing committee of Louisburg Square Proprietors, 193.

Gilmore, P. S., 141.

Gingko tree, 156, 157, 271.

Glapion, Louis, 219–33.

Glapion, Lucy, 224–32.

'Gleaner.' *See* Bowditch, Nathaniel Ingersoll.

'Gleason's Pictorial Drawing Room Companion,' quoted, 197–99.

Goldschmidt, Otto, husband of Jenny Lind, 201.

Goodwin, Mr., 82.

Goodwin, Eliza, agreement made by, with Proprietors' Committee of Louisburg Square, 192; quoted on the fountain in Louisburg Square, 195.

Grant, Moses, Sr., 180, 284.

Grant, Patrick, 96.

Grant, Mrs. Patrick (Anna Powell Mason), 96.

Grant, Judge Robert, 96.

Gray, Francis C., 178.

Gray, Harrison, 13, 85.

Gray, Horace, 212.

Gray, Samuel C., 207.

Gray, William, Jr., 105, 135.

Green, Abigail, wife of John Joy (3), 118, 121.

Green, Elizabeth, 121.

Green, Joseph, 121, 122.

Greene, Gardiner, 16, 32, 154, 156.

Greene, Mrs. Gardiner (Elizabeth Hubbard), 155–57.

Greene, John Singleton Copley, 137.

Greene, Mary, wife of Daniel Hubbard, 155.

Greene, Mary Anne, wife of Samuel Hubbard, 155.

Greenough, David, 206, 207, 259.

Gregerson, George, mariner, 260.

Grew, Henry, 138.

Grove Street, 213.

Guild, Curtis, publisher of the 'Commercial Bulletin,' 135.

Guild, Governor Curtis, 135.

Gun house, 77.

Gustine, Joel, 259.

Guttridge, Robert, 214.

Guttridge, Mrs. Robert (Mary Buttolph), 214, 248.

Hale, James W., reminiscences of, 46 *n.*

Hales, John Groves, plan of Boston by, 50, 233, 253.

Hamilton, William, 269.

Hammond, Samuel, 220, 254, 258, 264.

Hancock, Ebenezer, 148.

Hancock, Governor John, 20, 147; his heirs, 147, 148; widow marries James Scott, 148; elms on Common planted by order of, 271.

Hancock, John, son of Ebenezer, 148, 150.

Hancock, Thomas (1), uncle of Governor John Hancock, 20, 146, 147.

Hancock, Thomas (2), nephew of Governor Hancock, 150, 153, 154.

Hancock Avenue, 151.

Hancock house, 50, 119; torn down, 49; after Governor Hancock's death, 147; in hands of Ebenezer Hancock, 148; John Hancock in possession of, 150.

Hancock property, 20, 21, 146; constitution of, 147; the title, 147, 148; pasture lot bought by City of Boston, 148; formal division of, 148; lots made from, 149–59.

Hancock Street, laid out, 22; former names of, 22, 91, 114, 115, 215.

Hardy, Alpheus, 142.

Hardy, Mrs. Alpheus, 142.

Haskins, Thomas W., hardware dealer, 261.

Hayden, William, merchant, 239.

Heard, Henry R., treasurer of committee of Louisburg Square Proprietors, 194.

Heard, John, Jr., 185.

Heard, John T., clerk pro tempore

INDEX

Jordan, Eben D., Sr., 141.
Joy, Abigail, daughter of John (3) and Abigail, 118, 122.
Joy, Benjamin, member of syndicate, Mount Vernon Proprietors, 58–60, 82, 122, 275; Mount Vernon Street lot, 87, 92, 206; houses built by, on Chestnut Street, 88, 122, 123, 160–65; his career, 122, 123; deed to Jeremiah Gardner, 161, 162.
Joy, Mrs. Benjamin (Hannah Barrell), 60, 122, 164.
Joy, John (1), 121.
Joy, Mrs. John (Lydia Lincoln), 121.
Joy, John (2), son of John (1), 121.
Joy, Mrs. John (Sarah Homer), 121.
Joy, Dr. John (3), son of John (2), estate of, 22, 50, 91, 117–20; children, 118, 122; value of his property, 119, 120, 124, 127; sales of real estate, 119, 120, 124; his ancestry, 120, 121; arrangement with Mr. Perkins relative to building at No. 5 Joy Street, 131, 132.
Joy, Mrs. John (Abigail Green), 118, 121; removes to Mount Vernon Street, 130, 131.
Joy, John (4), son of John (3), 118, 122.
Joy, Joseph (1), 121.
Joy, Mrs. Joseph (Mary Prince), 121.
Joy, Joseph (2), son of Joseph (1), 121.
Joy, Mrs. Joseph (Elizabeth Andrews), 121.
Joy, Joseph Green, son of John (3), 118, 122.
Joy, Thomas, 120, 121.
Joy, Mrs. Thomas (Joan Gallop), 121.
Joy Place, Belknap Street, 134, 139–43.
Joy Street, early names of (Belknap, Clapboard, George, Joy Place), 12, 22, 91, 105, 114, 115, 134, 139–43, 214; named from Dr. John Joy, 50; Nos. 8 and 10, 92, 93; corner Pinckney Street, 94; corner Mount Vernon Street, 105–12, 120, 123, 149, 157, 158; origin, 113, 114, 279;

course, 114, 115; Nos. 1–5, 130–33 139–42, 159, 267, 269, 283, 289; incident relating to 'Jim' Fisk connected with, 143–45; tree at No. 5, 267, 269; tree on corner Mount Vernon Place, 267; house on, designed by Parris, 279; houses on, built by Coolidge, 283; No. 64, 283; window lintels in Nos. 1 to 4, 289.

Kendall, Thomas, tailor, 171.
Kimball, Fiske, book on architecture, 275, 286, 288, 290.
Kitchen Street (Branch Street), 170.
Knox, General, 56 n.
Kuhn, William P., clerk and treasurer of committee of Louisburg Square Proprietors, 194.
Kutts, John, architect, 259, 280.

Lamb, George, his real estate map of Boston, 3, 4.
Lancaster, William, bricklayer, 184, 248–50.
'Lane to the Almshouse' (Beacon Street), 17.
Lathrop, Reverend John, on the springs and wells of Boston, 34–40.
Lawrence, James, 139.
Lee, Nathaniel, 163.
Lee and Leighton, builders, 185.
Leverett, Governor John, 9.
Leverett, Knight, 240.
Leverett, Mrs. Knight, 240.
Lincoln, Amos, 82.
Lincoln, Mayor Frederick W., 189.
Lincoln, Joseph, housewright, 102, 179, 180, 278.
Lincoln, Lydia, wife of John Joy (1), 121.
Lind, Jenny, marriage of, 201.
Lindens, on Beacon Hill, 265, 267, 268, 271.
Litchfield, Ira, housewright, 246, 247.
Little, Brown & Co., office building of, 153.
Lodge, Senator Henry Cabot, 157, 211.
Lodge, John Ellerton, 157.

INDEX

INDEX

INDEX

ing up of north side of, 170; lots on north side of, 188; Nos. 48 to 56, 206; Nos. 69 and 71, 206; Nos. 5 and 7, Middleton-Glapion site, 218–35; north side of, between Joy and Anderson Streets, 233; No. 21, 234; Nos. 13 to 21, 234; Nos. 47 and 49, 234; No. 7, 235; No. 9, 235; No. 11, 235; No. 15, 235; corner Anderson Street, 256–58; Nos. 68 to 78, 259–61; as regards trees on, 264; tree in rear of No. 49, 268; ailanthuses on, 270; houses on, built by Lincoln and Stoddard, 278; No. 12, 278; house on, designed by Kutts, 280; flat-roofed houses on, 288.

Plumbing, 173, 174.

Pope, Ebenezer T., handcartman, 260.

Pordage, George, 15.

Pordage, Hannah, wife of James Bowdoin (1), 15.

Powder house, 9, 10.

Powell, Anna Dummer, second wife of Thomas Perkins, 106.

Powell, John, 106.

Powell, Mrs. John (Anna Dummer), 106.

Powell, Susanna, wife of Jonathan Mason (2), 85.

Powell, William, 85, 88, 89, 106, 107, 120.

Powell, Mrs. William (Mary Bromfield), 106.

Powers, Joseph, trader, 250.

Pratt, George L., 141.

Pratt, George W., 190; agreement made by, with Proprietors' Committee of Louisburg Square, 192; member of standing committee of Louisburg Square Proprietors, 193, 194.

Pratt, John, 258.

Pratt, Robert M., 190; member of standing committee of Louisburg Square Proprietors, 193.

Prentiss, Appleton, paper-stainer, 241, 242.

Prescott, William Hickling, historian, 139, 172.

Prices, of cotton goods, in early part of nineteenth century, 128; of land and houses, 63–65, 67, 68, 91, 92, 119, 120, 124, 127, 128, 130, 131, 147, 155–57, 166, 167, 172, 173, 177, 180–82, 189, 190, 207–12, 219, 238–44, 250, 253, 255, 258–61.

Prince, Mary, wife of Joseph Joy (1), 121.

Prouty, Dwight, treasurer of committee of Louisburg Square Proprietors, 194.

Pump, preserved, 138.

Quincy Market, 280.

Railroad, the first used in this country, 32, 80, 81.

Reed, Elizabeth, 190.

Reed, Reverend James, pastor of Church of the New Jerusalem, 190.

Reed, Sampson, expounder of doctrines of Swedenborg, 190; agreement made by, with Proprietors' Committee of Louisburg Square, 192.

Remick, Christian, drawing by, 'A Prospective View of Part of the Commons,' 51.

Render, Thomas, housewright, 92.

Reservoir, on Beacon Hill, 28.

Revere Street, 213; corner Anderson Street, 251–54; Nos. 33, 35, and 37, 252–54.

Reynolds, Harris A., 270.

Rice, Henry G., 173, 207, 209.

Richmond, Christiana R., 207.

Ridgway, Joseph, 13, 215.

Ridgway Lane, 215.

Riley, Michael, 228.

Rives, William C., Jr., 178.

Rockwood, Ebenezer, 96, 164.

Rogers, Annette P., 143.

Rogers, Daniel Dennison, 20, 106, 143.

Rogers, Henry Bromfield, son of Daniel Dennison Rogers, 106, 133, 142, 143.

INDEX

Rogers, Mrs. Henry B. (Anna Dummer Perkins), 106, 133, 142, 143.
Rogers, Isaiah, architect, 280.
Rogers house, 20.
Rollins, Eben, 152.
Rollins, Mrs. Frances Hicks, 152, 155, 156.
Rollins, John W., builder, 254.
Rollins Place, 254.
Roofs, 287, 288.
Ropewalks, 12, 22, 58, 77, 115, 215, 220, 234, 255.
Rowell, H. T., blacksmith, 246.
Russell, Benjamin, editor and publisher of the 'Columbian Centinel,' 224–31.
Russell, Nathaniel Pope, 125, 129, 137, 153, 155.

Sage, Ebenezer, 184.
Saint John's Church, Bowdoin Street, 237.
Saint Paul's Church, 279.
Salisbury, Samuel, 93, 95.
Salisbury, Stephen, Sr., 95.
Salisbury, Stephen, Jr., 164, 165.
Sanitary conveniences, 173–75, 208.
Sargent, Professor Charles Sprague, 140, 269.
Sargent, Ignatius, 140.
Sargent, Reverend John Turner, 207.
Sargent, Mrs. John Turner, 168.
Sargent, Lucius Manlius, paper on the Blaxton family, 203.
Savage, James, his 'Genealogical Dictionary,' 203, 204.
Savage, James S., agreement made by, with Proprietors' Committee of Louisburg Square, 192.
Savage, William, 154.
Sawyer, William, 206, 211.
Scholfield, Isaac, 234.
School, curriculum of, 257.
Schoolhouse, corner Pinckney and Anderson Streets, 256–58.
Scollay, William, member of syndicate, Mount Vernon Proprietors, 59, 60, 275.
Scott, Captain James, his connection with sale of Copley property, 59, 68, 69; marries widow of Governor Hancock, 148.
Scottow, Joshua, 12.
Scottow, Thomas, 12.
Scottow (Joshua) pasture, 12, 13, 214, 237.
'Sea level,' meaning of, 38.
Searl, Catherine, 52.
Sears, David, Sr., 19.
Sears, Colonel David, 55, 56 *n.*, 176–78, 210, 279.
Sears, Montgomery, 142.
Sears lot, 19.
Sentry Hill, 6.
Sentry Street, laid out, 28, 29.
Sewall, Joseph, 93, 95.
Sewall, Judge Samuel, 16, 22, 116.
Sewall Street, 116.
Sewall's elm pasture, 22, 116.
Shackleton, Robert, his 'The Book of Boston,' 291.
Shaw, Edward, architect, 280, 281.
Shaw, Gardiner Howland, 139, 159.
Shaw, Mrs. Gardiner Howland, 140, 159.
Shaw, Jesse, 184, 189; agreement made by, with Proprietors' Committee of Louisburg Square, 192; member of first standing committee of Louisburg Square Proprietors, 193; houses built by, 278.
Shaw, Chief Justice Lemuel, 94.
Shaw, Robert Gould, Sr., 139.
Shaw, Robert Gould, Jr., 178.
Sheldon, Asa G., 156; his autobiography, 7, 32.
Shepherd, George, 259.
Sherman, Nathaniel, 101.
Shillaber, Daniel, 228, 231, 232.
Shillaber, David, 227–30.
Shillaber, Mrs. David, 230, 231.
'Shinbone Alley,' 206.
Shippen, Edward, 15.
Shurtleff, Dr. N. B., 39.
Simmons, George W., 138.
Skinner, Francis, 136, 140.
Skinner, William Sutton, 124.
Smith, George G., steel engraver, 31.

307

INDEX

Town House, the first, 120.

Town plot, the, the lines of, 28, 29; sold by the town, 30.

'Transcript, The Boston,' 'Gleaner' articles in, 1, *see* Bowditch, Nathaniel Ingersoll; L. M. Sargent's paper on the Blaxton family in, 203.

Trees, on the Common, 157, 271, 272; streets named for, 263; age of, 263, 264; on certain streets, 264, 265; on private land, 265–71.

'Tremont,' origin of the word as applied to Boston, 6.

Tremont House, 280.

Trimountain, the, 6–8.

Tuckerman, Edward (1), 152, 155.

Tuckerman, Professor Edward (2), son of Edward (1), 152.

Tudor, Frederick, 139.

Tudor Apartments, 118, 130, 131, 133.

Tulip poplar tree, on Beacon Hill, 267.

Turner, Benjamin, housewright, 261.

Turner, Joshua, housewright, 261.

Turner, Robert, 18, 19, 21, 120, 147.

Turner lot, 18, 19, 21, 120, 147.

Turner Street (Hancock Street), 22, 91.

Tuttle, Daniel, brickmason, 171.

Tuttle, Julian, his suggestion as to the name Louisburg Square, 202.

Twentieth Century Club, 142.

Twist, Jonas, 243.

Twist, Solomon, 243.

Unitarian Society, 20.

Upham, Henry, 206, 209, 210.

Upham, Phineas, 190, 206, 209.

Upjohn, Richard, architect, 284.

Valley Acre, 14.

Vane, Sir Harry, 16.

Vassal, John, 17.

Viall, Mary, 26.

Vinal, John, schoolmaster and Justice of the Peace, his property, 51–56,

177; testimony as regards topography of Hill, 72.

Vinal, Judge, 56 *n.*

Vose, Elijah, 135.

Wadsworth, Alexander, treasurer of committee of Louisburg Square Proprietors, 194.

Wages of labor, in first half of nineteenth century, 32, 33, 82, 83.

Wainwright, Reverend Jonathan Mayhew, 136.

Wait, Josiah, trader, 246.

Waldo, Samuel, 215.

Walker, Nathaniel, treasurer of standing committee of Louisburg Square Proprietors, 194.

Wall, Captain John, 15.

Walnut Street, laid out, 79, 187; early nineteenth-century house on, 84; corner Mount Vernon Street, 119, 120, 123, 136, 137, 160; Phillips house on, 119, 127, 170; No. 14, 123, 286; Nos. 5 and 7, 124; Nos. 8, 10, and 12, 124, 125, 129, 134, 137, 138, 155; No. 6, 125; in 1814, 127; Nos. 2, 4, and 6, 134; Nos. 11 and 13, 179; as regards trees on, 264.

Walter, William, 96.

Ward, Samuel G., Jenny Lind married at his house, 201.

Ward, Thomas W., agreement made by, with Proprietors' Committee of Louisburg Square, 192.

Warren, Fiske, 159.

Warren, John C., agreement made by, with Proprietors' Committee of Louisburg Square, 192.

Washburn, Abiel, agreement made by, with Proprietors' Committee of Louisburg Square, 192.

Watch house, 77.

Watch tower, 9.

Watertown Arsenal, 280.

Webster, Daniel, 96, 212.

Weeks, Daniel, grocer, 181.

Weeks, Phineas, 259, 260.

Welch, Francis, agreement made by, with Proprietors' Committee of

309

INDEX